What Happened After the High

There are several familiar themes to questions that in‹
one thinks about the Highland Clearances.

There is a sense of moral outrage that leads you to wonder yet again: *how could* these lairds and their agents have been so cruel? There is no possible answer to that. And did any evictors regret their actions ? The answer to that is probably no.

The second theme concerns the extent of the clearances. How many people were evicted from how many areas? Where did they go? From the late 18th century to the 1850s, scores of estates, and tens of thousands of people, were cleared. The people were driven out to the coastal periphery, or had to make their way to the lowlands of Scotland or to England; or they were coerced onto boats and sent overseas.

The third theme concerns the aftermath. Did any of those poor evicted people ever return to the lands they once lived on? In other words, was anything ever done to *counteract* the clearances?

Many estates did become, and remain to this day, unnatural wildernesses. Yet some areas *were* indeed given back to the people, in the form of small crofts with common grazing land attached. The process took decades - far too long - but by the 1930s thousands of dispossessed Highlanders had moved back onto cleared lands.

Many were the descendants of those cleared earlier. And even a few very elderly people were able to experience the emotion of returning to live in areas from where they had been driven away as children.

One little-remembered public body was, in essence, given the task and the opportunity of beginning to reverse the effects of the Clearances. The Congested Districts Board for Scotland was set up by an Act of Parliament in 1897, to try to help those many Highland crofting districts in great need, some of them badly affected by evictions.

This Board did some good. But ultimately, tragically, it was condemned as a failure. A tremendous opportunity went to waste. Had a success been made of the Congested Districts Board, both at the drawing-board stage and during its active life, thousands more people would have remained in the Highlands during the last century, and many others who did cling on would have had their lives vastly improved.

The Highland Clearances

The grim saga of the Clearances is told in the books of Alexander Mackenzie, John Prebble, Eric Richards and James Hunter. It was Mackenzie who wrote these memorable words in his account of 1883: "There is nothing in history so absolutely mean as the eviction of the Highlanders by chiefs solely indebted for every inch of land they ever held to the strong arms and trusty blades of the progenitors of those whom the effeminate and ungrateful chiefs of the 19th century have so ruthlessly oppressed, evicted and despoiled." For mean, read vicious and immoral. The clearances could only be carried out because, technically, it was not illegal to evict Highlanders from the land which they and their ancestors had occupied for many generations.

Eric Richards wrote in his book *The Highland Clearances*: "The suddenness, and the almost total erasure of a highly distinctive society, distinguishes the Highland Clearances from the customary movement of other rural peoples from the land. ... A peasant society and a distinctive culture were, in many places, razed from the face of the land."

James Hunter wrote in *Last of the Free* of the terrible consequences of the evictions: "It was really a question of the survival of a distinct culture and identity and indeed whether the native people of the Highlands would remain in their own land."

To be sure, there were other struggling 'peoples' in the British Isles during the 19th and early 20th centuries - women, factory workers - but the fact was that the Gaels were truly a distinctive people, a race who came under sustained attack for decades.

As Ewen A.Cameron noted in his superb book *Land for the People*, the British Prime Minister William Gladstone wrote to his Home Secretary in 1885 that he believed the people of the Highlands had a historic title to land which had been usurped by proprietors for material gain. This was a wrong which should be redressed; for the rights of property in the Highlands came with 'engagements' in the shape of that history.

"For it is, after all," wrote Gladstone, "this historical fact that constitutes the crofters' title to demand the interference of Parliament. It is not because they are poor, or because there are too many of them, or because they want more land to support their families, *but because those whom they represent had rights of which they have been surreptitiously deprived to the injury of the community.*" The following year, Gladstone's Liberal Government pushed through the Crofters Act which at last stopped the threat of further Highland clearances.

Darkest Times

After a sickening wave of Highland clearances in the 1850s, fear held sway over thousands of West Highlanders who had no security over the little land they occupied and were completely at the mercy of lairds.

Potato blight had resulted in famine during 1846-47, and only a concerted relief effort by several bodies in the lowlands, latterly overseen by the Central Board of Management for Highland Relief (from 1847 to 1850), ensured the literal survival of thousands of people. Early in the famine, 200,000 Highlanders were deemed at risk of starvation. By 1848, nearly 70,000 still were. (However, this was nothing like as terrible as the famine in Ireland.)

At this time, a key member of the British government was Sir Charles Trevelyan, Assistant Secretary to the Treasury. As Professor Tom Devine puts it in his recent book *To the Ends of the Earth*: "Trevelyan's position was unequivocal. He regarded both Irish and Highland Celts as profoundly racially inferior to Anglo-Saxons. In his view, the potato famine represented the judgment of God on an indolent people who now had to be taught a moral lesson to change their values and attitudes so that they might support themselves in the future."

When the Central Relief Board was wound up in 1850, many landowners looked upon the near-destitute people living on their estates as a burden, and the option of 'emigrating' them began to appeal. Trevelyan and another public figure, Sir John McNeil, argued the case for a large-scale emigration of a 'surplus' Highland population. The Emigration Advances Act of 1851 provided loans at low interest rates to landed proprietors keen to 'encourage' people off their estates. Trevelyan became chairman of the Highland & Island Emigration Society, and recommended a programme to 'emigrate' 30,000-40,000 people from the West Highlands & Islands.

The Scotsman supported this goal, saying: "Collective emigration is .. the removal of a diseased and damaged part of our population .. it is a relief to the rest of the population to be rid of this part."

Arrested for Stealing Seaweed

During the dark decades of the 1850s and 1860s the people of the West Highlands must have felt they had no rights or protection at all. The law of the land was so much against them in even their most mundane efforts to survive.

In 1863 nine men from near Ullapool were formally prosecuted for cutting seaweed which they needed for manure, along the shores of Loch Broom.

The prosecution was brought at the instance of the Duchess of Sutherland (also the Countess of Cromartie) in an "Application for Interdict and Summons for Molestation and Damages."

It was solemnly asserted that Her Ladyship "had the sole right and property of the lands and barony of Coigach lying in the Parish of Lochbroom and County of Cromarty and had also the sole right and property of the pertinents of the foresaid lands and Seashore comprehending inter alia the Sea Weed or Wrack and Ware growing in the rocks and shore or washed up by the Sea" and that she was "entitled to exclude and prevent the defendant All and Each of them from trespassing and encroaching on the said lands and barony on the Sea Shore .. for the purpose of cutting gathering removing or carrying away any of the Sea Weed or Wrack and Ware and from cutting gathering removing or carrying away or interfering in any way with the said Sea Weed or Wrack and Ware or any part thereof or from doing any other act or deed on the said lands and barony or Sea Shore inconsistent with the Pursuer's rights ... And further that it might and should be found and declared that the Defenders by entering on said lands and Sea Shore and by cutting gathering and removing therefrom Sea Weed or Wrack and Wave had done wrong and committed manifest and violent molestation of the Pursuers And further that the Defenders .. be decerned and ordained to desist and cease from encroaching on the Pursuer's lands and from cutting gathering and removing or carrying away said Sea Weed or Wrack And further that the Defenders .. be decerned and ordained each of them to make payment to the Pursuers of the sum of £10 in name of damages."

That sum demanded of each man, £10, was a colossal amount of money at that time. For taking seaweed....

Even the native language of the Gael, as it became clear in 1872, had no official friends. The Education (Scotland) Act of that year prescribed education for all children up the age of 13 - which was a good thing - but it made absolutely no provision whatsoever for teaching Gaelic (or for teaching in Gaelic).

As a result, Gaelic was thenceforth actively discouraged in many Highland schools - to the point of children being beaten for using it.

The Crofters' War: The Bernera Riot

In 1874 on the island of Great Bernera, off the west coast of Lewis, there occurred one of the first cases of crofters rebelling in the face of an outrageous threat of eviction by Donald Munro, the factor of the Lewis estate of Sir James Matheson.

They had been asked to give up their common grazings (on the mainland opposite Bernera) to be made into deer forest, and in return would be given alternative grazings on part of the former farm of Earshader.

This they accepted, and they also complied with a request to build a seven-mile long dyke to separate the new grazings from the deer forest of Scaliscro. Then they were told they could not have that grazing land but were offered other land. The crofters objected.

In response, it was arranged that summonses of removal be served on them. During this episode a sheriff officer made a threat against some of the local children after they threw clods at him; the sheriff officer was rebuked and his coat torn. Three crofters were arrested and tried at Stornoway Sheriff Court – however, they were acquitted. Crofters were thereafter emboldened to complain to Sir James Matheson about Munro, who was dismissed a year later. It was a turning-point

John Murdoch: Inspiring Campaigner

In 1873 John Murdoch launched *The Highlander*, a weekly newspaper dedicated to the interests of the people. Murdoch, then aged 55, had grown up in Nairn, Perthshire and Islay and had a lifelong passion for the Gaelic language and culture. He had lately retired from a career in the Customs and Excise department, which had taken him all over the British Isles, including many years in Ireland, where he forged friendships with people who would later star in the Irish Home Rule movement.

Retiring to Inverness, Murdoch travelled throughout the Highlands in the 1870s while producing his newspaper, and one of his most famous pieces of writing in July 1875 included the following section:

"We have to record the terrible fact that, from some cause or other, a craven, cowed, snivelling population has taken the place of the men of former days. In Lewis, in the Uists, in Barra, in Skye, in Islay, in Applecross and so forth, the great body of the people seem to be penetrated by fear. There is one great, dark cloud hanging over them in which there seem to be the terrible forms of devouring landlords, tormenting factors and ubiquitous ground-officers.

"People complain; but it is under their breaths and under such a feeling of depression that the complaint is never meant to reach the ear of landlord or factor. We ask for particulars, we take out a notebook to record the facts; but this strikes a deeper terror. *'For any sake do not mention what I say to you,'* says the complainer. *'Why?'* we naturally ask. *'Because the factor might blame me for it.'* "

Murdoch also wrote: "The landlord class in the Highlands have been but the usurpers of the right which the people there once possessed in the soil."

After Murdoch's *Highlander* newspaper folded in 1881, the Gàidhealtachd was fortunate that another fine campaigning journalist and author was at hand in Alexander Mackenzie, a Gairloch man whose publications *The Celtic Magazine* and *The Scottish Highlander* filled the void. Mackenzie published his most famous book, *The Highland Clearances*, in 1883, and so brought those grim events into the public eye.

Skye Troubles

In 1877 the Kilmuir estate in Trotternish, Skye, doubled the rents which it charged to crofting tenants. The land belonged to Captain Fraser, originally from Nairn. His factor collected the new rents with some difficulty, with many crofters at first offering partial payment. After being threatened with eviction and a refusal to supply them with seed, they paid in full, but attitudes were beginning to harden.

Three years later, tenants on the east side of the estate around Staffin began to withhold the increased portion of their rents. They were led by Norman Stewart, a Valtos crofter and fisherman. Stewart had served a week in prison for taking heather and rushes from the moor to re-thatch his house, something which still rankled. He began agitating for reform and was nicknamed 'Parnell' after the Irish Nationalist leader. In 1877 he had refused to pay the rent increase initially but eventually had relented. In 1880 there was some confusion over the valuation of his croft, and Stewart again refused to pay in full - and was soon joined in this by other crofters. In 1881 the landlord Captain Fraser tried to sway local opinion by sending out packets of tea and sugar to the poorest crofters of Uig, Staffin, Kilmuir and Culnacnoc.

Two weeks later he arranged for the factor to issue eviction warnings on the agitators especially 'Stewart at Valtos'.

On Easter Monday in Glasgow a public meeting was addressed by the president of the Irish Land League, Parnell himself. The meeting passed a motion in support of the tenants threatened with eviction in Valtos, pledging support 'whatever form the struggle might take'.

Further public meetings passed similar motions; the crofters now had many friends in the lowlands. Captain Fraser held a meeting with the tenants and both sides accepted a reduction in rents. The crofters had their first taste of what militant action could achieve.

Braes

Then another serious dispute broke out in the Braes south of Portree. A group of young local crofters had recently returned from a fishing trip to Kinsale in Ireland where they had become familiar with the Irish land struggle.

Back home in Skye, they and their fellow crofters drew up a petition for the return to common ownership of grazings on Ben Lee which had been seized for sheep-farming by the proprietor, Lord MacDonald. Until this concession was granted, they would refuse to pay their rents. In December these became due for payment, but no Braes crofter arrived to settle up at the factor's office in Portree.

On April 7th 1882, Sheriff Officer Angus Martin headed to the Braes to serve summonses for eviction of the ringleaders. As he approached with his retinue, two boys appeared in the distance and ran off, only to reappear carrying flags, whilst other boys ran ahead to warn the remaining crofters. Soon a crowd had gathered, and Martin and his men were surrounded by an angry mob. The summonses were snatched away and burnt in front of the Sheriff Officer, who retreated to Portree.

The summonses were dropped, but warrants were issued for the arrest of those obstructing Martin and burning the orders. Martin wrote to William Ivory, sheriff of Inverness, saying that one hundred soldiers needed to be stationed in Portree to keep order.

On 19th April, forty policemen arrived from Glasgow and together with Sheriff Ivory marched to the Braes. They arrived at 6am and arrested the five ringleaders.

The alarm was raised, however, and 300 Braes men descended on the police as they took their prisoners back to Portree. They launched a volley of stones, whilst the police fought back with truncheons. Women both dealt and received blows, with seven of them being seriously injured by the police. By means of a final charge the police managed to break through and escape with their prisoners. The newspapers dubbed it 'The Battle of the Braes'. Today the spot is marked by a memorial reading 'Near this cairn on 19th April 1882 ended the battle fought by the people of Braes on behalf of the crofters of Gaeldom'.

The trial of the Braes men was held in May without the usual jury, and they were found guilty and imprisoned. Soon, however, sympathy for the men was growing in the cities; newspapers were outraged and several MPs demanded an inquiry.

Glendale

Unrest spread almost immediately to Glendale in Duirinish. The crofters there, led by John MacPherson, were demanding the return of the common grazings of Waterstein. By May several crofters had begun grazing their cattle on the land, and court orders issued for their removal were ignored. In November one of the estate shepherds tried to removal the cattle, but he was assaulted by their owners. By Christmas, warrants were issued for the arrest of twenty Glendale men involved in the assault, and on 16th January 1883 four policemen were dispatched to stations around the area. A large crowd had assembled to meet them, and the police were beaten and driven back to Portree. By 20th January, even the regular constables stationed at Dunvegan had fled their posts.

Incredibly, an official government emissary was then sent to Skye aboard a navy gunboat to negotiate with the Glendale men. It was agreed by the government that a Royal Commission would be set up to investigate the crofters' grievances, and in return a token five crofters agreed to stand trial. They became known as the Glendale martyrs, MacPherson among them, and are commemorated by a memorial in the district today.

The Napier Commission

In 1883 the Liberal Government ordered the setting up of a Royal Commission of Enquiry into the conditions of crofters and cottars in the Highlands.

Under the Chairmanship of Lord Napier, it began taking evidence in May, from crofters around the Highlands and Islands, as to the conditions under which they lived and the sufferings they had endured. The other members of the Commission comprised landowners Sir Kenneth Mackenzie of Gairloch and Donald Cameron of Lochiel, Sheriff Alexander Nicholson (son of the proprietor of the Skye estate of Husabost), Donald Mackinnon, a Colonsay man who was the first Professor of Celtic at Edinburgh University, and Charles Fraser-MacKintosh, MP for Inverness Burghs who had long spoken out for the crofters' best interests.

Hundreds of ordinary Highlanders had the chance to speak at sittings of the Commission – many were encouraged to speak out by John Murdoch and Alexander Mackenzie, who would travel to areas which the Commission was about to visit and rally them to attend.

The Commission's eventual report became a historical - and historic - landmark in its recording of endless cruelties and abuses perpetrated by lairds and factors against Highland people over many decades.

The Commission made various recommendations: notably that the traditional system of township be adopted, whereby all settlements of three or more holdings with common pasture, or with a history of such within the past forty years, should be classed as townships. Among other suggested reforms was one that tenants with holdings valued over £6 in annual value should be given a secure tenure and a lease, while those with holdings of less than £6 in annual value should be encouraged to emigrate.

Alexander Mackenzie criticised the Napier Commission's report for not recommending security of tenure for all crofters and cottars, nor any provisions for crofters' landholdings to be extended.

Meanwhile the Highland Land League (HLL – slogan: *The People are Mightier than a Lord – Is Treasa Tuath na Tighearna*) was growing in membership and attracting support from fledgling socialist groups across Scotland. Rent strikes broke out in several parts of the Highlands and Islands.

During 1884 there were discussions in Parliament as to what legislation would satisfy the majority of crofters. In 1885 the Liberal Government prepared a Crofters Bill (very similar to the one of the following year) but it was not passed as the government fell. A minority Tory Government took over. Meantime the HLL announced its intention to put forward candidates for Parliament in every Highlands and Islands constituency - and they won four seats at the election of late 1885.

That election brought in William Gladstone's third Liberal administration, with the support of 86 Irish Nationalist MP's. During its very brief period in office, the Government would focus on the proposed Irish Home Rule Bill but also (before it fell in the summer of 1886) the Crofters Holdings (Scotland) Bill.

The Crofters Act

It was this Act which, at last, after so many decades of arbitrary evictions by landlords, effectively prevented any further Highland clearances being carried out. Its coming into force was a close call, for Prime Minister William Gladstone's Liberal administration of that year barely had time to pass the Act before it fell. The Crofters Act became law on 25th June 1886.

For the first time, thousands of crofters were given security of tenure. The Crofters Commission, established under the Act, quickly began to review the rents of crofters and reduce them greatly; while also reducing or cancelling many crofters' rent arrears. The Crofters Commissioners numbered three men – Sheriff David Brand, W.Hosack and P.B.Macintyre – who together made a huge improvement to thousands of lives over the years that followed.

A century after the passing of the Crofters Act, J.F.M.MacLeod, then Chairman of the Crofters Commission, paid tribute to John Murdoch and to William Gladstone in the introduction to a book about the great campaigner: "Had John Murdoch not agitated, and had Gladstone not legislated, it is exceedingly doubtful if there would have been a crofting population in 1986."

However, the 1886 Act had a great failing in that it did nothing for the thousands of landless people known as cottars, nor did it give the Crofters Commission any powers to create new holdings for such people. But cottars desperately needed land; and the Highlands were still in dire need of infrastructure and facilities such as roads and piers.

Therefore, what was required was further legislation to address all these needs: either through giving the Crofters Commission additional powers or through establishing a new body to address these tasks.

It would take eleven long years after the passing of the Crofters Act for the next piece of legislation.

Meantime the first adjudications of the new Crofters Commssion were announced early in 1887, and they brought welcome relief. Kilmuir crofters were astonished to be given rent reductions of about 40%, and to have on average two-thirds of their rent arrears written off. Captain Fraser might still be the landlord but he could no longer rule the people at his own whim.

Meantime cottars drew attention to their desperate plight by carrying out land raids on farms on Lewis, at Park in 1887 and Aignish in 1888.

Congested Districts Board Set up in Ireland

The Congested Districts Board in Ireland was established by the British Government under Arthur Balfour in 1891, to encourage economic and social development in the poorest districts of the West, North-West and South-West of the country. The following summary is from the University of Cork.

"Arthur Balfour, Chief Secretary for Ireland, driven by his conviction that state paternalism was necessary to remedy the special problems of isolation, poverty and unemployment that affected the West of Ireland, established the Congested Districts Board in his Land Act of 1891.

"The Board was staffed with sympathetic and well-informed persons and it was given financial independence. Its purpose was to develop the West of Ireland. It surveyed and identified the problems. By 1901 it was responsible for an area of nearly 3.7 million acres inhabited by half a million people."

"From 1909 the Irish Congested Districts Board had a large annual budget of £250,000. It set about improving the economy by financing the infrastructure and subsidising the introduction of new industries and agricultural products. It purchased land for tenants and re-distributed it in economic holdings. In fact, it bought over 2,000,000 acres of land from which it created or improved 60,000 farms. It spent a total of £2,000,000 on improvements to land, houses, farm buildings, drainage, roads, and fences.

"It encouraged a wide range of cottage industries - bee-keeping, spinning, knitting, crochet, lace-work, carpentry, kelp-making - and taught invaluable skills, for example, in domestic economy, poultry and egg production, and horse-breeding. Among the successful industries encouraged by the Board were Dripsey Woollen Mills, Foxford Woollen Mills, and Killybegs Carpets.

"It employed agricultural instructors to advise farmers. It vigorously promoted the fishing industry: it built piers, gave capital grants to fishermen for boats and tackle, and introduced marketing strategies. The sales of fish more than trebled between 1891 and 1913. Michael Davitt, who ironically described the Board as 'enlightened state socialism', wrote: 'though opinions differ as to the amount of good done by this body there can be no doubt that much benefit has been conferred by its labours upon the several districts comprised within its area'.

"In many ways the Board was the ancestor of all modern regional development agencies, a highly advanced government body of a kind not seen elsewhere in the United Kingdom in these years."

One member of the Irish Board from its inception until 1923, when the Congested Districts Board was dissolved by the Irish Free State and its functions transferred to the Land Commission, was Rev. Patrick O'Donnell, who had become the youngest Catholic bishop of his time in 1888. Born in Donegal, he was hands-on in his work with the CDB, even commissioning a carpet factory in Killybegs to make an altar carpet with a Celtic design for a new Cathedral in Letterkenny. He later became Archbishop of Armagh, and then a Cardinal. O'Donnell's close relationship with the people of the congested districts of Donegal, most of them Gaelic speakers like him, gave the CDB a measure of credibility in the county.

In 1898 the United Irish League (UIL) was launched with the motto "The Land for the People". It sought land reform compelling large grazier farmers to surrender their lands for redistribution amongst small tenant farmers. Founded and initiated at Westport in County Mayo by the former MP William O'Brien, by 1900 it had expanded to include hundreds of branches across Ireland.

In 1909 the area in Ireland defined as congested was expanded and the CDB was given increased powers under The Irish Land Act. During the time of the Irish CDB, the land question was always alive in the national consciousness.

The Deer Forest Royal Commission

In Scotland, a Congested Districts Board was still some years in the future at the time the Irish Congested Districts Board was set up, in 1891. However, in that year there was at least further helpful legislation in the form of the Western Highlands & Islands Works Act. This made provision for the construction of roads, piers, and other useful works in the more remote and neglected areas.

The Act followed the West Highlands & Islands Commission of 1889-90, which recommended (among other proposals) the extension of railway lines from Fort William to Mallaig, from Strome Ferry to Kyle of Lochalsh, and a new railway to Aultbea in Wester Ross (unfortunately the latter line was never built). By an annual vote of Parliament thereafter, £20,000 was made available to the newly established County Councils to be spent on infrastructure projects.

In 1892, County Councils were also given limited powers to acquire land to use for smallholdings under the Small Holdings and Allotments Act. However, Councils within the Highlands showed little enthusiasm for using this Act to tackle the huge challenge of making land available for cottars.

The Deer Forest Royal Commission was established by Parliament in 1892 to enquire what land in the Highlands, presently reserved for deer-stalking, would be suitable for crofting.

In 1895 it presented its report, noting that 794,750 acres of land in the Highlands were suitable for the creation of new crofts, while 439,188 acres of land were suitable for extending croft holdings. In other words, the land was there for landless people.

Certain members of the Commission added in their final report that "the profitable cultivation or advantageous occupation of the scheduled lands could only be obtained under a well-considered scheme of land purchase by a representative body possessed of full powers for carrying out properly penned regulations, both as to the selection of tenants for new holdings and also as to the occupation of all grazings scheduled." (J.P.Day, *Public Administration in the Highlands & Islands*)

The Commission drew criticism for taking three years to produce its findings. Had the Government then acted on those findings by passing legislation allowing a public body to make compulsory purchases of that identified land to be given over to crofting, that would at least have vindicated the Commission's efforts.

The Liberal Government did, in fact, promote a Bill to address the needs of cottars in 1895, but it was gradually watered down before the government fell anyway.

It was the incoming Tory government which, two years on, brought forward legislation in the form of The Congested Districts (Scotland) Act.

The Congested Districts Bill in Parliament
Last-minute Pleas for Powers of Compulsory Purchase
In June 1897, as the CDB Bill was debated in Parliament, there were last-minute pleas to the Government to addres its glaring defect - the lack of powers of compulsory purchase. Hansard reported a speech by Ross & Cromarty MP Mr J.G.Weir, who warned the Government that the Congested Districts Bill "would not settle the Highland question. The people wanted to be reinstated on the lands which were occupied by their forefathers, and which were now used for deer and sheep.

"According to the Report of the Deer Forests Commission, there were nearly 2,000,000 acres of land in the Highland crofting counties suitable for the occupation of crofters, cottars, and fishermen. ... Large as the scope of this Bill was, it required powers the absence of which would tend to make it unworkable so far as the extension of holdings was concerned. It contained no compulsory powers for the acquisition of land. .. The Commissioners under this Bill would have their hands tied in the case of an unwilling seller.

"Take, for example, the island of Lewis, with its population of nearly 30,000 living under the most difficult conditions under one proprietor who might be unwilling to sell. Only last autumn, when in Lewis, the Hon. Member introduced to the proprietor a deputation of County Councillors and other leading inhabitants of the island who were desirous that land should be provided for the creation of fishing villages in the neighbourhood of the bays where fish abounded, as well as for sites for cottars, and the extension of crofters' holdings.

"The proprietor of the island declined, however, to meet the difficulty. .. For want of compulsory powers to obtain land, the Congested Districts Board would be foiled on the very threshold of their work. Would the Lord Advocate consider the advisability of providing a remedy to meet this glaring defect in the Bill?"

Examining the proposed composition of the Congested Districts Board, Mr Weir suggested that all three of the current Crofters Commissioners should be on it - not only the chairman David Brand, but his colleagues Messrs Hosack and Macintyre.

"With regard to the constitution of the Board, two of the proposed members, the Chairman of the Local Government Board and the Chairman of the Fishery Board, were located in Edinburgh. These gentlemen could not spend, say, eight or ten days in travelling to and from remote parts of Lewis, Harris, the Uists, or Barra - the very districts where congestion was most keenly felt. He suggested that all the three Crofters Commissioners should be members of the Board, and he did so because these gentlemen had a thorough practical knowledge of the grievances of the Highland people, every acre of land in all the crofting counties, and the value of land in the respective districts."

Even the MP for Hawick Burghs in the Scottish Borders could see the terrible defect of the Congested Districts Bill and how it would fail the people of the Highlands:

"The substantial taking of land would form the key to the success or failure of the Bill as a whole. But Section 5 was practically an optional and not a compulsory taking of land. If a proprietor in the Highlands was willing to sell, all that Section 5 did was to give a means by which the arbitration should proceed under the Lands Clauses Act. Upon that point he hoped the Government would listen to an appeal which he now ventured to make. He asked them to produce some clause or clauses that would give compulsory power for taking land for the purposes of this Bill. The safety of such taking was well assured. The taking of land would be in the present case at the instance of a composite and great public Board for the great public weal of a large part of Scotland, and in these circumstances he thought the Government should take a stronger line than they had taken, and affirm by statutory enactment that such Board, finding themselves in a position to declare that the land was required, should have the power to put down its foot and say to a recalcitrant proprietor that he must concede what was for the public weal in regard to this matter of land."

Another MP, Mr Caldwell, commented that the Bill "gave money for the purchase of seed and for the erection of fishermen's houses and other purposes. *But how could they build fishermen's houses if they had no compulsory powers to enable them to acquire land? He considered the Government ought to make the power of acquiring land compulsory and not voluntary.*"

The Congested Districts Board (Scotland) is set up

The Congested Districts (Scotland) Act came into force on 6th August 1897. The sub-heading of the Act defined it as being "to provide for the administration of Sums available for the Improvement of Congested Districts in the Highlands and Islands of Scotland."

The Act's main purpose, therefore, was to spend money: in order to "improve" congested districts. A few paragraphs below, these sums were specified as £35,000 annually, comprising £15,000 which was to be taken from a pot available under the Agricultural Rates, Congested Districts, and Burgh Land Tax Relief (Scotland) Act of 1896, plus a sum "not exceeding £20,000" to be voted annually by Parliament.

This was not new money. As Ewen A.Cameron has pointed out, this £20,000 had been made available since 1891 under the West Highlands & Islands Works Act, and was now re-directed to the CDB each year.

The only other funding available to the CDB was to be "any moneys received for payment of interest or repayment of principal of any loan made by the Commissioners" plus "any other sums applicable to the purposes of this Act".

The CDB was, quite simply, inadequately funded from the very start, and this was to cripple it. £35,000 per annum was a drop in the ocean – around £4 million in today's money, and not enough to make a major difference to crofters' and cottars' lives quickly. The funding available to the CDB was to be given out either as a gift or a loan, and with the following eight goals in mind - of which the third and fourth were the most challenging and promised to make or break the Board's reputation.

"(a) aiding and developing agriculture, dairy farming, and the breeding of livestock and poultry in congested districts; and

"(b) providing suitable seed potatoes and seed oats and implements and dairy utensils and machinery or appliances for the making of butter or cheese for crofters and cottars in congested districts; and "(c) providing, subject to the provisions herein-after contained, <u>land for sub-division</u> among or for <u>enlargement</u> of the holdings of crofters and cottars in congested districts for the purposes of cultivation or grazing, in such manner and upon such conditions and after such adaptations as shall be determined by the Commissioners; and

"(d) aiding <u>migration of crofters and cottars</u> from congested districts to other districts in Scotland, and settling any migrants under favourable circumstances in the places to which they first migrate; and

"(e) aiding and developing fishing (including industries connected with and subservient to fishing) and the erection and formation of fishermen's dwellings and holdings in congested districts; and

"(f) aiding the providing or improving of lighthouses, piers or boat-slips, public roads and bridges, and footpaths and foot bridges, and meal-mills, in congested districts; and providing guarantees for telegraph extensions, or such other postal facilities (including money order and savings bank business) as may be within the power of the Postmaster General to grant under guarantee; and

"(g) aiding and developing spinning, weaving, and other home industries in congested districts; and (h) subject to the consent of the Treasury, aiding the providing or improving of harbours."

Apart from its inability to make compulsory purchases, the CDB also lacked other important powers. Most notably, it could not make grants or loans to allow crofters to purchase livestock.

A Part-time CDB

The CDB Act noted that there should be 5-8 Commissioners on the Board, including the Secretary for Scotland as Chairman, along with the Under Secretary for Scotland, the Chairman of the Local Government Board for Scotland (that was the body charged with overseeing local government, public health and poor law in Scotland from 1894 until 1919, when it was replaced by the Scottish Board of Health), the Chairman of the Fishery Board for Scotland, the Chairman of the Crofters' Commission, and up to three other persons to be nominated by the Secretary for Scotland. The running of the whole show was very much in his hands:

"The Secretary for Scotland may from time to time make, alter, and vary such rules as he shall deem necessary for regulating the proceedings of the Commissioners, and the times and places of their meetings."

Unfortunately, the members of the CDB rarely met together face-to-face. They were part-timers. Even the secretary, a key figure, was appointed, as the Act stipulated, from another Scottish department and served the CDB only in a part-time capacity.

This was a key deficiency of the CDB: for how could part-timers seriously hope to address the desperately pressing needs of the Highlands and Islands?

Consider the example of the Under-Secretary for Scotland, Colin Scott-Moncrieff, who had spent much of his career serving the British Empire as an engineer in India and Egypt. In 1892 he had been appointed Under-Secretary for Scotland and permanent head of the Scottish Office. Based in Whitehall, he would occasionally travel by train to Edinburgh for short visits during which as many duties as possible had to be crammed into his schedule.

Scott-Moncrieff wrote from Edinburgh on one such visit: "I have been very busy since I came down, or at least very fully occupied, for I'm not sure that the out-turn of work is very great. I have inspected three great prisons, and the big Morningside Asylum; talked fisheries, sheriffs' courts, destitution in Shetland, smallpox, etc."

Perhaps the poor Shetlanders deserved more of his time. Scott-Moncrieff's colleague Sir James Miller Dodds later wrote of him that he was also a member of the Local Government Board for Scotland and had to advise on matters affecting the application of the Poor Laws, referred from Edinburgh for decision, and to keep in touch with the growing problems of housing and public health. He was also on the Board of the Scottish Prison Commission. His niece, Mary Rollings, later recalled: "... he was never sorry when business took him to the office in Edinburgh, where, after travelling all night, he would work all day, the second morning finding him once more at Whitehall."

He may have been well-meaning but clearly such a busy public figure was not able to give his undivided attention to the needs of the Congested Districts.

Deciding whether a Parish was a Congested District

Right from the outset, it was left to the Congested Districts Board's small staff in Edinburgh to sort out the definition of what actually constituted a "congested district". A list of such districts was not specified in the Act.

The CDB had a remit to help the seven crofting counties of Argyll, Inverness-shire (which then included Skye, the Uists and Harris), Ross & Cromarty (which then included Lewis), Caithness, Sutherland, Orkney and Shetland. These included over 150 parishes; but some had few or no crofters, notably on the east coast of Inverness-shire and Ross-shire, and the Board felt it need not deal with them, however poor they were. The CDB also had to be mindful of its budget, which was so limited, which led to its excluding certain "better-off parishes" from its assistance, even in crofting areas.

In deciding whether the genuine crofting parishes of the west and north would qualify for help, the CDB used the following calculation as its test: the valuation of the parish divided by the local population. If this figure did not exceed £1.00 per person per year (exclusive of rents obtained from shootings and from holdings rated at over £30 per annum, and exclusive also of the population on these holdings), then the parish was congested and CDB assistance could be offered. So a figure for the total valuation of each parish was obtained; and then that was divided by the population.

Dating from 1899 (two years after the CDB was set up) is a file in the Board's records (AF42/450) which includes various calculations as to whether a parish was congested or not. Thus, the parish of Applecross easily qualified because its total valuation was £1,585 8s 8d, while its population was 2,038 - giving a valuation per person of only 16s 3d (about 82p).

Neighbouring Lochcarron, however, was excluded from the list of congested districts, because its average valuation was over £1.00. Lochcarron was not therefore officially congested.

Yet for some reason several exceptionally poor west coast parishes, whose average valuation per head of population was under £1, were not allowed onto the CDB's qualifying list. These parishes included Glenshiel (population 394, valuation per head 10s 6d. or 52½p), Morven (population 820, valuation 10s 9d. or 54p) and Jura (population 724, valuation 12s 1d or 60p).

As of 1900, the following 56 parishes were recognised as Congested Districts; their populations, where given, were noted in the above CDB file.

Argyll: Kildalton & Oa (on Islay) – population 2,027; Kilchoman (on Islay) – pop. 2,697; Kilfinichen & Kilvickeon (includes Iona and south-west Mull) – pop. 1,735; Torosay (Mull); Kilbrandon & Kilchattan (the only qualifying parish on mainland Argyll) – pop. 1,574; Tiree – pop. 2,452.

Inverness-shire: Glenelg *(the only parish on mainland Inverness-shire to qualify)* – pop.1,503; Small Isles – pop. 436 *(this included Eigg, Canna, Rum and Muck – Eigg having the main crofter population,the latter two islands having no crofters)*; all seven parishes of Skye, viz. Sleat – pop. 1,850, Strath – pop. 2,392, Portree – pop. 3,176, Kilmuir – pop. 2,394, Snizort – pop. 1,908, Duirinish – pop. 3,933, and Bracadale – pop. 920; and four Outer Hebrides parishes, viz. Barra – pop. 2,365; South Uist – pop. 5,821; North Uist – pop. 4,187; and Harris – pop. 5,024.

Ross & Cromarty: three parishes on the mainland, viz. Applecross - population 2,038; Gairloch – pop. 4,181; Lochbroom – pop. 3,910; and all four parishes on Lewis, viz. Lochs – pop.6,432; Stornoway – pop. 11,800; Uig – pop. 3,660; and Barvas – pop. 5,699.

Caithness: Reay - pop. 2,075; Dunnet - pop. 1,488; Watten - pop. 1,390.

Sutherland: Assynt – pop. 2,551; Eddrachilles – pop. 1,409; Durness – pop. 960; Tongue; Farr – pop. 1,857; Lairg - pop. 1,169; Kildonan - pop. 1,828: Loth – pop. 528; Clyne – pop. 1,713; and Dornoch *(landward area only, not the town of Dornoch)*.

Eight Orkney parishes and nine on Shetland were also declared eligible for the CDB's assistance. These 56 parishes had a total population of around 100,000. In terms of the average valuation per person in 1899, the poorest parishes were Lochs

(5s 11d), Barvas (6s 8d) and Durness (7s). Some parishes were more heavily populated than others, and so could expect more help from the CDB over the years.

In the Dark about the CDB

In its first months, the CDB was unsure whether it might yet be able to offer some assistance to any parishes which it had not officially recognised as congested. In December 1897 the Board received an enquiry from Orkney, written by Samuel Lindsay, convener of the Burray Proposed Pier Committee:

"Sir, Would you please explain to me in a word what a "Congested District" implies? I have read and re-read the Congested Districts Act but have failed to fully understand its meaning as it applies to the above question."

The CDB Secretary, R.R.MacGregor, then wrote to the Secretary for Scotland:

"The real difficulty of answering Mr Lindsay — otherwise than by a reference to section 10 of the Congested Districts Act – is that of premature publication of the policy of the Board – at least until a decision has been come to about works in parishes that are not "congested" – i.e. are above £1 per head."

In other words, there was difficulty not only in deciding which parishes were congested but in deciding whether that was the only crucial yardstick.

Even the CDB was in the dark about the CDB.

There should have been a sense among people in the crofting counties that the legislation of 1897 was a great step forward and an Act to *reverse* previous clearances. There should have been notices in the press, with a Gaelic-speaking representative appointed in each county. Instead, many people in 1897 and for several years thereafter, were not even aware that the Act had come onto the statute book.

Early Days: Distress on Barra

From the Congested Districts Board's inception in 1897, it had only a small staff based at its office on George Street, Edinburgh. The same few names recur constantly in the Board's extensive records (now held at the National Records of Scotland).

The Congested Districts Board began its active life in September 1897. File number one concerned Bayble Pier: the clerk of Ross & Cromarty County Council asked the CDB to take over a commitment to assist the building of the pier, previously given under the 1891 West Highlands & Islands Works Act. The CDB agreed.

In 1899 the CDB was notified that there was great distress on Barra. It was an example of the Board's not being geared up to act quickly enough in such a case, that a protracted correspondence ensued, involving the Secretary for Scotland Lord Balfour of Burleigh, Chairman of the Fishery Board Angus Sutherland, Chairman of the Crofters Commission Sheriff Brand, Vice-President of the Local Government Board Malcolm McNeill, and the Secretary of that same Board Mr Falconer-Stewart.

The whole tone of this correspondence was almost discursive, with comments being telegraphed between Board members scattered around the country. Meantime, on the ground in Barra, people were needing help urgently.

Falconer-Stewart wrote to the CDB in February saying the County Medical Officer for Inverness-shire had written that the local Inspector of Poor had told him the previous November that there was more distress on Barra now than at any time in the past forty years. Falconer-Stewart then wrote for clarification to the Inspector of Poor on Barra, Angus MacDonald.

Sutherland minuted that it might be useful to fund public works on Barra such as a pier at Brevaig, while MacNeill suggested the construction of roads as a way of providing employment - the CDB, he felt, ought to "be prepared with the bones of a scheme for turning out the whole male population if an emergency should arise." He suggested asking the Crofters Commission to undertake the upkeep of a pier at Brevaig if it was built, and to carry out a survey of the local roads.

The Under Secretary for Scotland harked back to his colonial experiences in administering India: "we should keep ready by us the project of some useful work to be started in Barra at a time of need. This is part of the Standing Policy of the Famine Department of the Government of India, with which I am very familiar. Every district officer is required to keep all cut and dried in his office a useful work which may be at once started, should scarcity arise. If it would be a good thing for Barra it would probably be equally good for other islands."

Angus Sutherland wrote that he agreed with MacNeill: "If we took up the Brevaig pier we would have to go on with it, while the Local Government Board wish to have a card up their sleeves for the Wilsons & co, so to speak."

This comment about *"the Wilsons & co"* referred to Thomas Wilson, who was already becoming well-known to the CDB as a staunch campaigner for the interests of the people of Barra and South Uist. As early as October 1897 he had written his first letter to the Board, in his role as solicitor and clerk to South Uist Parish Council, enclosing this excerpt from recent council minutes: *"It was agreed to ask the County Council to direct the attention of the CDB to the pressing necessity of giving early attention to the requirements of South Uist..."* and listing six urgent projects, comprising a boat slip at Eriskay, a telegraph service to Eriskay, three roads, and a school footpath. (Later Thomas Wilson would work for the CDB.)

In 1900, Wilson wrote again about conditions in Barra, which led to a report on conditions on the island being compiled by Mr MacIntyre of the Crofters Commission.

That in turn drew two extraordinary and self-justifying reports from Lady Gordon Cathcart, who owned Barra and the Uists. One report is 15 pages long, the other 45 pages long, and both are held in CDB files. It is impossible to read them without anger at this woman who held the quality of life of the local crofters and cottars in her hands, and who had refused so many of their appeals for land;   and whose late father-in-law Sir John Gordon of Cluny had ordered some of the very worst, most brutal evictions from Barra and South Uist in the early 1850s.

Land Purchases

The CDB, as mentioned, had no powers to undertake compulsory purchases of land. It was instead to negotiate with landowners who expressed a willingness to sell land.

The relevant section of the CDB Act noted: "Acquisition, adaptation, and disposal of land. ... Any limited owner may sell land to the Commissioners for the purposes of this Act, at such a price, or for such consideration as, having regard to those purposes and to all the circumstances of the case, is deemed reasonable; a limited owner may also, with the sanction of the Local Government Board given under this section, convey the land for that purpose either without payment of any purchase money or compensation, or at a price less than the real value, and may so convey it free of all incumbrances."

The Congested Districts Board was to adapt and improve its landholdings by means of sub-division and fencing, making roads, and providing drainage and water supply, prior to selling them. And the CDB could erect buildings for settlers:

"The Commissioners may also, if they think fit, adapt the land for the purposes of this Act by erecting or assisting in erecting thereon such buildings, or making such adaptations of existing buildings, as, in their opinion, are required for the due occupation of the land, and cannot be made by the crofters or cottars or fishermen."

As it turned out, the CDB's policy was to expect settlers to build their own houses and outbuildings.

Land Purchase as against Tenanting

The Act showed that one of the expectations of the CDB would be to re-sell lands which it had purchased. It was always the plan that after estates had been bought up and made suitable for crofters and cottars to move onto, they would be sold to them – not outright, but over, for example, a fifty-year period.

However, the CDB discovered that most crofters did not aspire to own the holdings which they occupied.

As J.P.Day explained: "What influenced the crofters was the fear of the ownership rates. A croft valued at £100 might be in the occupation of a crofter paying £5 annual rent with all the advantages of the statutory crofting tenure. Should he purchase this croft, he would be called upon to pay the Board's purchase annuity of £3 14s 1d. annually for fifty years.

"This saves him about 25 per cent per annum for 50 years and then gives him free possession, but on the other hand, if owners' rates were five shillings in the pound, this saving would be wiped out, and if rates were higher, as they frequently are, he would be left at a positive disadvantage. As a crofter and occupier of an agricultural holding, he could only be assessed at three-eighths of the occupier's half of the assessment on his fair rent, although he might have put up on the croft superior buildings of considerable annual value. As an owner he would be liable to be assessed, both as owner and occupier, on the full annual value of buildings and land, with a deduction of five-eighths of the agricultural value qua occupier only.

"The crofters, accordingly, were afraid of an increased valuation, and were unwilling to purchase unless the margin between the Board's purchase annuity and the fair rent were large enough to provide for owner's rates and for any increased rates both on owner and occupier which might result from an increase in their valuation. As the Board point out, this condition could not be fulfilled in most cases unless the State resold at a greatly reduced price, a policy involving regular and perhaps considerable loss on each transaction.

"Matters were rather at a standstill as the Board were under the impression that they could only sell their lands and not lease them. In 1908, however, the CDB was advised by the Law Officers of the Crown that it was competent for them to lease land out."

It was incredible that it took the CDB eleven years to understand this point.

Migration

One principal aim of the CDB Act was to encourage migration away from congested districts. However, this would prove to be virtually unattainable.

There was, in fact, a fundamental difference between the Board's wishes and the people's wishes, summed up in this comment from a Board report of 1900:

"Those who ought to become migrants are often very reluctant to leave their homes, such as these are; and those among whom it might be proposed to introduce such migrants are not always willing that the experiment should be tried. Again, many of those prepared to migrate will not, or cannot, quit their present abodes unless the whole expense of migration and re-settlement were borne for them.

"There are large numbers of cottars in certain townships who pay little or no rent, and who form a serious incumbrance to the crofters, but who could not be migrated on any other terms. Moreover, they would not undertake the burden of any loan, but would look to obtaining pecuniary aid in the form of a gift.

"Even if a loan were arranged, the task of obtaining repayment might easily become insuperable. Nor can it be left out of view that migrants who, from whatever causes, did not succeed in their new holdings, would look to the Board to save them from destitution.

"The difficulty in such cases of altogether rejecting a plea for .. aid and making everything turn on self-reliant and independent effort would be very great. It ought, further, to be stated that in certain quarters where schemes of migration might

properly be entered upon, there is no available land, or at least none to which the migrants would be willing to go."

That year, the people of the township of Sconser on Skye had refused to migrate to Suisnish and Borreraig just a few miles away, where better land had been made available for them. Although not many miles distant, these lands held no appeal for the Sconser people. Suisnish may have been regarded as tainted ground, its people having been cleared in 1853, as memorably described in a passage by the geologist Archibald Geikie, who stumbled on the community on the day of the clearance.

Highlanders' resistance to the idea of being pressured to move was entirely understandable. The clearances are rightly seen as an abomination partly because they had up-rooted people from a land and culture and history which they held very dear. The CDB Act may have stressed migration rather than emigration – that is, a move to another part of the Highlands - but it missed the point that the Gael is deeply attached to his own homeland.

The CDB also noted with regret that those who might be prepared to migrate would only do so if the full costs of their resettlement elsewhere were to be paid – which seems a fair request.

On the other hand, ironically, when 28 crofters and 21 cottars at Breanish on Lewis did ask to be moved in 1906, and the local proprietor was willing to sub-divide the farm of Dalbeg for them, it was the CDB and Crofters Commission which frustrated the scheme by deeming the land unsuitable. Three years later, the proprietor offered land at nearby Mangursta, and thirteen applicants from Breanish were at last given new holdings.

Co-operating with Proprietors to acquire Land

The Congested Districts Board did make some positive early progress when it concluded negotiations to sub-divide two North Uist farms owned by Sir Arthur Campbell-Orde at Sollas and Grenitote during 1898-99.

The results of this first experiment in breaking farms into crofts was actually quite successful: Sollas being divided into twelve holdings at £10 annual rent and Grenitote into 22 holdings at £5 annual rent. Twenty-five cottars and nine crofters were established in the new holdings, and the removal of the latter gave opportunity for the enlargement of seven old crofts. The Board's help was £845 spent on roads and fencing etc, and £310 in loans to settlers for house-building. By 1912 the settlers had paid up all annuities due, and there were no arrears.

There was also an experiment in erecting fishermen's smallholdings and dwellings at Battery Park, Stornoway, where land was purchased in 1899 to create 29 lots, which were all occupied by 1906.

In 1898 CDB members discussed the estate of Glendale in north-west Skye. P.B.Macintyre, working for the Crofters Commission, had reported in April on the lands of Waterstein, Lorgill, Glen Dibidale and Glen Ollisdale, part of the estate of Glendale and the property of Mr Hugh MacPherson. Eight new holdings could be formed at Waterstein, suggested Macintyre. In May the Secretary for Scotland noted "This report is not encouraging as regards forming holdings for crofters." Sir Kenneth J.Mackenzie of Gairloch discussed possible rates of repayment by crofters.

At this time it was a key part of CDB strategy that any estates which it purchased would in turn be re-sold, rather than leased. (Glendale would, in fact, be acquired by the Board in 1904.)

How to Spend the CDB's Budget

In March 1900, the secretary of the Congested Districts Board sent an estimate of receipts and payments for the coming year (1900-01) to the Under-Secretary for Scotland at Whitehall, asking the Treasury's approval of the estimate.

The way this sum was broken down reveals the CDB's priorities. The estimate for receipts comprised the annual £35,000 guaranteed, plus another £2,060 from bank interest etc. Lighthouses, piers etc were allocated £14,000. Land and migration was also allocated £14,000 - of which £10,000 was proposed to be given out in loans and £4,000 in grants & other expenditure. Agricultural grants etc was allocated £3,781, and the construction of certain piers £2,368. Administrative expenses included £350 for the engineer & his staff; agricultural inspector £100; clerks £161; and travel expenses £800. There was £750 for the maintenance of minor lights; while home industries (grants & other expenditure) were allocated £300.

Despite the CDB being associated in Highland history most particularly with land purchases for the creation of crofts, it is evident from the above list that works on the ground absorbed a large part of its budget.

A year later the Congested Districts Board's secretary Mr MacGregor noted that the *actual* expenditure had been rather more. In explanation, he commented:

"As you are aware, it is difficult to estimate with assurance expenditure in certain of the sub-heads where much depends on the applications made to the Board, and the opportunities afforded to them of exercising their powers, e.g. in the settlement of crofters on land. The excess of £944 10s 2d in grants and other expenditure in Agriculture was mainly caused by more extensive outlays on stud animals than was contemplated, while the excess of £4,224 15s 8d under Land & Migration is owing to the Board having purchased land in Barra as well as the Sutherland estate they had in view."

Syre and Barra

These land purchases involved the first major undertakings by the CDB. 12,116 acres at North Syre in Strathnaver, Sutherland, were lotted in 1900 into sixteen considerable holdings designed to be self-sufficing. These attracted an insufficient number of applicants able to provide capital to take over the valuation stock, so the land was subsequently re-lotted into 29 units and sold to 23 settlers.

The other purchase was of 3,000 acres at Eoligarry, Barra, which was sold in twenty-five agricultural and thirty-three smaller fishermen's holdings.

The idea was that these settlers should purchase their new holdings, but this was another failure of the CDB's overall strategy. Few settlers wanted to buy. In 1912, in the final year of the Board, a unanimous request from all Syre and Barra settlers was received, that they might revert to being tenants, and this request was granted. In the same year the Glendale crofters also applied to the new Board of Agriculture for Scotland to revert to being tenants in order to avoid liability for owners' rates, but the Board managed to persuade them that it was not to their advantage to do so, owing to the favourable terms on which they were buying their holdings.

Need for Roads

In 1900 the Crofters Commission prepared a report for the CDB on the agricultural condition of every congested district, "specially with a view to the improvement of the crofters' stock and the best means for reducing the over-stocking that is so prevalent".

The report also addressed the issue of roads and communications. Of the parish of Applecross it was noted: "A road from the terminus of the present road at Applecross through the crofting townships along the west and north of the estate and continued to the Lochcarron road at Shieldaig, would prove a great boon."

It reflects very badly on the CDB and on its successors that this road was not constructed until *over seventy years later*. The section between Shieldaig and Kenmore in 1970, that between Kenmore and Applecross in 1976.

This failure to grasp how vital roads were was highlighted in the story of crofter Calum MacLeod of Raasay, who eventually gave up hope of any public body ever providing a road to his own declining township at the north end of the island, and did the job himself. Roger Hutchinson's brilliant book *Calum's Road* tells that remarkable story.

St Kilda - Making a Real Difference

St Kilda occurred frequently in CDB files around the turn of the century. A new pier was built by the local community with grants and guidance from two resident supervisors of works employed by the CDB.

The local people were paid to do the construction work. However, a dispute over who was to do what during the building was reported in June 1900 following an inspection by Colonel James Gore-Booth, Consulting Engineer to the Scottish Office. He noted:

"Mr Wookey *(a local CDB supervisor)* has had great difficulties to contend with as regards the Natives and has shown great tact and firmness. ... When I arrived Mr Wookey reported that the men had been practically on strike and had actually taken away the capstan belonging to the works. I at once ordered a meeting of the people and by help of a sub-agent of the proprietor's *(MacLeod of MacLeod)* I was able to speak to them. After saying I was disappointed at the way they had behaved I ordered them to replace the capstan at once. As they showed hesitation I repeated the order still more peremptorily with the result that the capstan was re-fixed in five minutes. I then gave the order for them to man the boats to land 20 tons of cement,

"At first they hesitated but on my threatening that if they did not obey I would withdraw the Supervisors and leave the work altogether or get outside labour to complete it, they complied and set to work. The result of this threat had the desired effect."

Gore-Booth's visit to St Kilda cannot have been very long, and yet he felt entitled to make extremely general and disparaging remarks about the people, as follows:

"I must say I was not favourably impressed with the inhabitants. They seem idle, shifty and not particular as to what assertions they make or the least ashamed to be found out in their statements. They are dirty in their habits, and their cottages (on the outside) simply stink. All sorts of garbage and filth festering about their doors. It would be very difficult I fear to get them to improve but it might be tried."

This report drew another patronising comment from the CDB's Malcolm MacNeill, who minuted: "The cause of the trouble was manifestly the same as that which produces difficulties with (say) African native porters, viz. an attempt to 'try it on,' and the remedy which has been found effectual in this case has equally succeeded in the other: More Education!"

In 1901, with the pier completed, St Kildans William MacDonald, Norman McQuien (sic) and Neil Ferguson sent a letter to Colonel Gore-Booth, copied to the CDB. This was in response to a letter from the Secretary for Scotland Lord Balfour of Burleigh, commending the people for their good work on the pier.

"St Kilda, July 25th 1901. Sir, We the undersigned committee appointed by the people of St Kilda to take charge of the sheds, tools, boats etc, beg on behalf of the whole of the inhabitants of this island to offer you our best thanks and assure you of our deepest gratitude to yourself and the Congested Districts Board for the generous treatment we have received at your hands, both during the erection of the Pier and in presenting us with the tools, boat etc. We were all surprised when Mr Wookey [CDB local supervisor] *read your letter to us, for Mr Fiddes* (the St Kilda minister) *had not said anything of having received a letter from Lord Balfour of Burleigh. We thank you too for the kind way you speak of our work at the pier. It is the first time any of us have been engaged in*

Kentangaval, Barra *(George Washington Wilson)*

*any work of the sort and we are very glad to know you can speak so well of us.
Mr Wookey has done his best to teach us, and what we have learned from him
will be the greatest benefit to us, all our lives.*

*"We enclose some rules which, with the assistance of Mr Wookey, we have
drawn up and now submit to you for approval and beg to say that if you wish to
add anything to them, we shall be only too glad to insert the same. We propose
to start a Fund to which all will contribute for the upkeep of the tools etc, also
to add to the list as we are able. In reference to the pier we had always been told
no pier could be put on St Kilda and we had given (up) hopes of ever having any
landing place but the rocks.*

*"The danger we always stood in the launching or landing, is now past, and
everyone on the island joins in thanking you for that and all the other kindnesses
you shewed them and received from you, and they will be gratefully remembered
as long as our descendants are on this island.*

*"We also feel proud to be able to point out for our children such a result of
their fathers' labour. It is the greatest benefit that has ever been conferred on
us."*

The construction of the St Kilda pier must surely have brought a glow to the
hearts of all at the CDB. Having read this letter, Angus Sutherland noted:

"I take a sort of paternal interest in this pier, and I expect to be presented with
the freedom of St Kilda some day. I wonder if this spontaneous letter had much
judicious preparation? What could the Rev Fiddes have in his eye in withholding
Lord Balfour's letter from the unsophisticated natives?"

Sadly, 29 years later the last of the islanders would be evacuated from St Kilda
at their own request, as the CDB's successor the Board of Agriculture would
record. This, the remotest of all the communities that the CDB had dealt with,
was by then simply no longer able to sustain itself.

In 1901, four years after the Congested Districts Board was set up, it asked the
Lord Avocate for an opinion as to whether it could legitimately buy land which
was already partly under crofting tenure.

The CDB had observed that its Irish counterpart was now purchasing estates
which were already partly under fixed tenure and was encouraging tenants to
give the Irish CDB's officers full liberty to "re-stripe the land in the manner
which appears to them most advantageous to the occupiers."

The Lord Avocate in Scotland informed the CDB that it could go ahead in such
cases.

Such observations of the work of the Irish CDB occurred regularly. The Irish
Board was the model on which the Scottish body had been based.

Idrigill by Uig, on the CDB's Kilmuir lands *(George Washington Wilson)*

Tiree: Prime Example of the Cottars' Crisis

CDB records for 1901 contain the following letter sent by the Duke of Argyll to the cottars on the island of Tiree - which he owned. It is self-explanatory and given here in full, and it demonstrates how regrettable it was that the CDB had not been given powers of compulsory purchase under its own Act.

Reading it, even now 110 years later, one can only reflect on the misfortune which the poor cottars of Tiree endured in living under this regime.

"To the Cottars of Tiree. Inveraray, May 1901.

"Gentlemen, I have received letters within the last month, all couched in the same terms, regarding a desire to possess small Holdings, showing that these letters coming as they do from different places, have been written under the guidance of your advisers. It will be well, therefore, to reply to you at once, so that all may have the same answer to the same demand.

"I am convinced from the experience of the past, as well as from recent observation, that a family cannot be supported in any comfort on any small patch of land, such as is usually known by the name of an allotment, in our climate and on our west coast land. A fair sized croft is necessary, and land for large sized crofts is at present not available. They who have not got that must turn to fishing, or other employment elsewhere.

"On the Argyll estates on the West of Scotland, the allotment system has been very fully proved. You know that during the War with France, the Argyll farms were divided into small crofts, and given to those who would serve, and whose tenure was that they should serve in wars. Land would not otherwise have been given except with the obligation to serve.

"Now, the system of small crofts failed because men grew dependent on the potato and barley or oats, and if these failed they were often on the verge of starvation. Small crofts were therefore gradually made into bigger ones that could sustain a family. Even were the whole island of Tiree divided into small holdings the relief would be very temporary if all those born on the island got holdings. The number of people is now greater than it was a century ago, though much less than it was after the potato had been grown, and when the kelp trade flourished.

"As potatoes often fail and the kelp trade is no longer of much value, it is evident that other resources must be tried, and that men must not be dependent on the land alone. You should enlist in the Naval Reserve, which will give every man some money and will let you see something of the world outside Tiree. It is true that there is not much work offered in Tiree, but in all other places men seek work where they can get it. They do not wait for it to come to them. When the potatoes failed after 1840 more than 200 Mull and Tiree men offered themselves for work and worked in Kintyre. There are very many lowland farmers anxious to get workers now, and all desiring it can learn where work is wanted through my office, or newspaper offices.Fishing should help you, especially if you work like the East Coast people in boats of some size with a crew obedient to a skipper. This is how the East Coast people succeed in catching far more fish than do our people.

"It has been proposed that each of you should put £10 or £20 into a fishing boat, and then I might help you as I have done before, that you may work like the East Coast men under a skipper, and share the catch according to your money.

"Whenever an opportunity occurs I am willing to see if patches for vegetables can be given to industrious men employed in the fishing – but all cannot have patches of land. This relief is not likely to be of immediate avail, but I am also willing to assist in getting good land for those who may like to join their friends in New Zealand or Canada. There I have seen men who had as little as you have at home, well off, with good houses and many fields of fine crops belonging to them.

"If men come to you, or write to you saying 'you should ask for land to be given to you', you may ask them in what part of Europe this is done. Progress can only be made by following where there is employment to be obtained, and if it can not be had in one place, there are plenty more where honest labour will fetch its good price. You have your houses free of all rent for the land on which they stand, but as for garden land, if any can be obtained from the present possessors, you will be liable to be charged something for it, and it is only the industrious, who would not be dependent on such patches, who could be accommodated.

"I am, your obedient servant, Argyll"

This letter was evidently copied to the CDB, for it is still in one of its files. One can only hope that CDB members who read it felt frustration at their inability to instigate an immediate process of compulsory purchase of suitable land on Tiree to give to these unfortunate cottars.

They deserved nothing less than a few acres each of the Duke's colossal estate.

The CDB in 1902: Judgment Reserved

In 1902, W.C.Mackenzie wrote in his *History of the Outer Hebrides* the following comments about the Crofters Commission and Congested Districts Board:

"Insufficiency of land and insecurity of tenure were largely responsible for the inertia of the people, and for the primitive conditions under which they were content to live. Their spirits were broken by the oppressions of the past, and their energies were paralysed by the uncertainties of the future. The land problem in the Long Island is still in process of solution, and may yet, possibly, present difficulties which will tax the resources of wisdom and statesmanship.

"When the history of the land question in the Highlands is written, it will form an economic treatise of surpassing interest and value. It will trace to their real sources, such incidents as the Bernera riots in Lewis in 1874, and the sporadic outbreaks in other parts of the Outer Hebrides since that date. It will describe the operations of the system which preceded the passing of the Crofters Act in 1886, and the intolerable conditions which made remedial legislation inevitable.

"It will give a faithful record of the splendid work performed by the Crofters Commission, under many difficulties, discouragements, and obloquy. *It will criticise the timorous mandate, and analyse the multifarious ties, of the Congested Districts Board, whose work concerns the Outer Hebrides more than any other locality.*

"The work of this Board is being watched with sympathetic interest. Whether its tentative efforts to cope with the demand for land, and to improve the agricultural and general conditions in the congested areas, will achieve, with the enlargement of its powers, and with the spread of education, the ultimate settlement of the land question; or whether its experiments will merely pave the way for the introduction of legislation which shall aim at finality; in either case, all who deplore the evils of congestion in the Long Island, and who desire to see the people in healthier homes, and leading happier and more prosperous lives, will wish success to this, and to all other agencies of melioration."

It may be mentioned that those long-awaited histories of the land question have been written in recent years by James Hunter, Ewen Cameron and Andy Wightman.

Crofter Life under CDB Ownership - Glendale

In 1904 the CDB became the proprietor of two very large estates on Skye, and appointed for the first time a full-time land manager, based at Uig, Kilmuir, who was to administer all the Highland estates from Barra to Syre.

The Glendale estate comprised 20,000 acres, including several crofting townships - home to some 160 crofters and cottars. Kilmuir, at the north end of the Trotternish peninsula, comprised 45,000 acres, with a number of established farms, which were to be broken up for crofts, as well as existing crofting townships such as Staffin, Duntulm and Idrigil. The total rent arrears owed by the 450 Kilmuir crofters to the previous landlord were over £4,000. This was reduced by the Board at the time of the estate's purchase to just over £1,000.

The CDB, as mentioned, hoped to persuade crofters on its various estates to purchase their holdings rather than rent them. Ultimately, however, only the Glendale people agreed to buy their land, on a fifty-year payment plan. Most crofters balked at the thought of risking the security of tenure which they enjoyed as tenants, and feared not being able to re-sell their land - at the same time knowing that their rates might increase.

Angus MacKintosh, the CDB's new land manager (or factor), was a native Gaelic speaker from Daviot, Inverness-shire, who had since 1901 been employed as factor to Lady Emily Gordon Cathcart on Barra and South Uist. Having started his new job, MacKintosh took it upon himself to file special reports on all four of the CDB's main properties. These provide an interesting snapshot of the challenges facing those who had been given land by the Board. The factor's report on Glendale in October 1904 begins thus: "On arrival at Dunvegan I called for MacLeod of MacLeod, who kindly agreed to accompany me to Glendale so as to introduce me to some of the people. We called for Mr MacDonald, the shooting tenant, and went on to Waterstein to see John Gillies the Farm Manager. We also saw John MacPherson, Lower Milovaig, Mr James MacRaild, Ground Officer, Colbost, and others."

John MacPherson had been the leader of the Glendale community during the land agitations of the 1880s.

A meeting of the whole Glendale community was convened at Borrodale School. "Before addressing the meeting I had short interviews with the people of each township in a separate room for the purpose of ascertaining their attitude with regard to the Club Farm and as to certain proposed changes affecting the individual townships." Club farming was then seen as an important way of allowing crofters to share stock according to their finances.

The report went on to summarise the creation of planned new holdings at Waterstein and discussed which crofters were willing or able to be moved, as well as practical details of fencing, house repairs etc. It emerged that seven Glendale crofters, who lived in Colbost, Fasach and Glasphein, were keen to move to Kilmuir - presumably because the land there was considered so good. Thus: *"Donald Stewart, No.17 (Colbost), would like to remove but would prefer to go to Kilmuir than to Waterstein."*

MacKintosh, like the CDB in general, placed great importance on the income derived from fishing and shooting tenancies. At that Borrodale meeting, he had asked the shooting tenant Mr MacDonald to address the community.

"He complained of unfair treatment at the hands of the people, particularly with regard to the fishings as there had been a great deal of night poaching on the river, and he intimated his intention of giving up the place in consequence."

And further on it is noted: "As to the fishings, I think the people realise how important it is to put a stop to all poaching and that they will do their best to bring that about." He suggested the present ground officer Mr MacRaild be kept on as a 'local correspondent', having been employed by the Glendale estate for forty years. "John MacPherson strongly recommended having a local man."

Crofter Life under CDB Ownership - Syre

Regarding Syre, which had been the CDB's first major investment in land, it was noted that at this time the 29 lots were tenanted by 23 crofters, who had moved inland to Syre from the Sutherland coastal townships of Kinlochbervie, Eriboll, Tongue, Bettyhill, Strathy, Melness and Golspie. (No fewer than 12 of the 23 tenants were named MacKay.)

Commenting that several tenants were struggling, MacKintosh was rather blunt. Of Robert MacDonald at no.10, who had been a joiner in Tongue, he wrote

"MacDonald was well spoken of in Tongue and he impressed me rather favourably but from what I could learn of him since he came to Syre he does not lead me to believe that he will make a successful settler. He is ready to give a dozen reasons to show why he cannot succeed for every one in favour of the colony. He is a shrewd young fellow fond of writing and talking and it is feared he may unsettle some of his neighbours who are plodding away and making the best of a stiff uphill struggle. If he is as he says quite convinced that he cannot succeed, the sooner he leaves the better for himself and for the Board."

Robert's brother Donald, also an ex-joiner, was at no.24 and also attracted negative comments: "MacDonald is a nice quiet lad but he lacks the energy and grit required for a place of this kind. He has given up all hopes of succeeding and it is most improbable that he will do so. He, like his brother Robert at no.10, has his trade to fall back upon and I should imagine he would do far better by following it than at farming which he does not understand nor take kindly to. I do not think he should be encouraged to remain."

Of Angus Gunn at no.18 (another joiner), it was noted: "Gunn did not impress me favourably as likely to make a good successful settler. He is on bad terms with both his neighbours and is said to be causing unrest and dissatisfaction among the other tenants. If he could be induced to go it would be a good thing for all concerned."

It reads strangely now that certain recently arrived tenants should be encouraged to leave. Was this not premature? Should the granting of a croft on this CDB estate not have brought with it the same respect for their tenure that most crofters had legally enjoyed since the 1886 Act? The trouble with that Act was that only crofters who had qualified at that time were protected.

MacKintosh concluded that ten of the 23 tenants at Syre "may be regarded as doing very well", and a further seven "may be said to be doing fairly well and likely to survive if they persevere and do not lose heart". But six tenants were deemed unlikely to succeed "and an understanding should be come to with them without delay."

Of these he noted that: "No.8 (George MacKay) is already away and has left nothing behind him but a badly built corrugated iron erection to meet the advances made to him amounting to £200. No.10 will probably agree to go quietly but there may be some difficulty in getting him to square up. No.15 (Murdo MacLeod) would leave if he knew where to go to. No. 25 will also, I think, agree to go quietly. No 26 &27 (John MacKay) says he cannot stay but we may have some difficulty nevertheless in getting him to go. Mr Chisholm (no.29, former Syre farm manager) thinks there will be no difficulty in getting good men to take up vacant crofts."

MacKintosh noted that the local shooting tenant was not happy with the effect of the Syre settlement on his season and had singled out one crofter for scuppering the killing of a stag due to his wandering about the hillside - looking for a missing stirk, the crofter later said, while apologising.

It was, admittedly, in the crofters' interests to look after the shootings, because they each received a share of the shooting rent – seven guineas per croft.

Crofter Life under CDB Ownership - Barra

In the factor's report on Barra, filed in November 1904, he made personal comments once again but did not reveal that he knew all the Barra people already from his days as the factor for Lady Gordon Cathcart. He had visited the island that month with the CDB's engineer, Walter Coles. These two men would, over succeeding years, between them lay out many hundreds of crofts.

The factor commented favourably on the two west side townships of Grean and Cleat, but found fault with matters on the east side, at Northbay, Bayherivagh, Bogach and Ardvernish. "The state of matters in these townships flavours very much of concerted inaction and the settlers appear to have been hanging back in the hope of being allowed to continue indefinitely in the temporary huts they now occupy, or to compel the Board to erect their houses for them, or pay them for preparing and collecting stones.

"Many of these settlers are undoubtedly in very poor circumstances. They had very little ready cash when they entered the holdings and the little they had they spent in erecting their temporary dwelling houses. Since then, the fishing industry in these waters has been very unremunerative and it has been a struggle with most of them to "keep the wolf from the door". The winter fishing for the last two seasons has been a failure and the prospects for the coming season are anything but bright. A number of the men who went to Glasgow to seek employment were unsuccessful in finding it and had to return home. Almost the only means of livelihood they have at present is that of cockle gathering.

"In these circumstances it is not altogether surprising that little has been done, but, on the other hand, had they devoted even one day a week to preparing building materials they would have had a sufficient quantity collected by this time." The factor had a talk with each man and at the end "they almost without exception undertook to make a beginning now and to let me see on my next visit that the period of inaction had come to an end."

Ten crofters, comprising five at Ardvernish, one at Northbay, three at Bayherivagh and one at Bogach, were " reported to be hopeless, or nearly so, but, in view of their undoubted poverty and the earnest promise now made, I would respectfully recommend that they should get yet another chance…" But the factor suggested the removal of two other crofters: one from Northbay and one from Ardvernish. The former had his old house at Bruernish available "and his removal might have a good effect on the others."

This report also touched on a controversial sixty-acre potato ground on Vatersay which the CDB had bought from Lady Gordon Cathcart several years earlier. The ground appeared, on inspection, suitable for potatoes, but many complaints had been received. "I made enquiries of several people, including the Piermaster at Castlebay, who all informed me that the crop for the past two seasons has been almost an entire failure." The factor suggested that in 1905 a variety of seed should be obtained from the Vatersay farmer or from South Uist, and that a soil sample might be analysed. "It occurs to me that as the land is a narrow promontory extending into the sea and is continually watered by its spray the soil may be excessively impregnated by salt."

Once again, MacKintosh did not mention that he knew the lie of this land as he had been Lady Gordon Cathcart's factor when the ground was sold to the CDB.

CDB: The First Eight Years in Review

The Congested Districts Board's report for the year to 31st March 1905 reviewed its activities to date. Nearly £250,000 had now been spent: of which £113,600 (nearly half) on land purchases; £7,000 on loans to settlers for buildings; £31,000 on developing lands; and a further £8,500 on smaller (but vital) projects such as fencing.

Other principal outlays were on public works: including £44,000 on roads, bridges and paths; and £44,000 on marine works such as piers, boat slips and sea walls.

Glendale had been purchased for £15,000 at public auction in December 1903, with the date of entry fixed at Whitsunday 1904. Plans were being drawn up to "re-sell the property to about 160 settlers in small holdings." The purchase of Kilmuir had been agreed in January 1904 for £80,000, though certain legal proceedings had delayed the final transfer of ownership to the CDB until November.

"We have since then been engaged in carrying out arrangements preliminary to a sub-division of the available lands as current leases of the large farms come to a termination." New croft holdings had also been created elsewhere, at Glenelg and at Kall, North Uist. The report noted: "A number of proposals have been made to us during the year for the purchase of land and also to aid proprietors in the sub-division of farms for the settlement of crofters and cottars in holdings near their present abodes in the congested areas."

In the past year the CDB had also purchased 45 bulls, 100 rams and 12 horses to be used for breeding purposes by crofting townships.

John Sinclair, Secretary for Scotland

During the lifetime of the CDB various Secretaries for Scotland were in office. Each in turn acted as Chairman of the Congested Districts Board.

The one who lasted longest was Lord Pentland. As plain John Sinclair he took on his new role in 1905, under the incoming Liberal Government, and he would stay in post until 1912 - becoming Lord Pentland from 1909.

Still a relatively young man, Sinclair was a former soldier who had taken a degree in law after leaving the army and then been elected MP for Forfarshire.

He was by instinct a reformer. In education, he oversaw acts enabling the provision of school meals and school medical supervision, as well as education for handicapped children.

But the subject dearest to his heart was the land. He sympathised with land raiders, and felt they had moral rights which needed to be matched with legal rights. For years, he championed a bill to extend small landholdings to more people throughout Scotland.

First brought forward in 1906, the Small Landholders (Scotland) Bill aimed to provide for the enlargement of existing holdings, if not by mutual consent, then by compulsory powers, but its passage was thwarted in the House of Lords for five years. This delay in its becoming law was to damage the credibility of the CDB.

Kilmuir and Glendale - to Lease or to Sell?

In July 1905, several members of the CDB including R.R.MacGregor, secretary, Angus Sutherland, chairman of the Fishery Board, and Sheriff Brand, chairman of the Crofters Commission, paid a visit to Kilmuir, where they "considered as to the adjustment of several matters requiring attention." *(Scotsman.)*

One particular priority was to confer with as many crofters as possible on the estate in order to ascertain whether they would agree to purchase either their existing holdings or new holdings in course of being formed from the farms on the estate. Well-attended meetings with crofters were held at Kilmuir, Staffin and Uig.

"The circumstances attending purchase, and the consequences, were fully expounded at each meeting, both in Gaelic and English and, moreover, a statement was read setting forth these circumstances in detail. It was finally arranged that a synopsis of the statement should be printed, both in English and in Gaelic, and circulated amongst all the crofters on the Kilmuir estate, and a full opportunity afforded them for considering the terms before requiring any final answer to the proposals laid before them by the Board.

"It may be mentioned that at each meeting a considerable number of questions were put and answered, from which it appeared clear that the crofters of Kilmuir fully understood the situation, and will consider carefully the ultimate course they will adopt."

They did just that. And their verdict was not what the CDB wanted.

In May 1906 *The Scotsman* noted with respect to Kilmuir: "We learn that the Kilmuir tenants have been raising trouble. …the crofters there have been listening to evil counsellors, and have received with abuse an offer which would make them absolute owners of their crofts at the end of a term of fifty years, on payment of an annual sum less than the present fair rent."

This was, in effect, the beginning of the end for the CDB's cornerstone policy of selling on its landholdings rather than keeping them to be leased out.

The Crofters Commission's annual report of 1906 reviewed its achievements during the twenty years since the passing of the Crofters' Holdings (Scotland) Act. The Commission had now assigned 49,038 acres of increased holdings, although recent annual totals were very small (only 23 acres in the past year). Rents payable by crofters had been reduced during those twenty years from a total of £83,681 to £62,006 - a reduction of nearly 26%. The Commission had also cancelled rent arrears totalling £124,185, two thirds of the total (£184,999) reviewed - testimony to how punitive previous rents had been.

The Scotsman, commenting on this report, was interested in Glendale:

"No direct light is thrown upon the land raids and other disturbances, actual or threatened, which have been reported from certain parts of the Outer Hebrides. There is, however, more than ordinary interest attached to the notes on the services the Commission were asked to render, outside their ordinary duties, in giving information and advice to the Congested Districts Board, which has purchased the estates of Glendale and Kilmuir in Skye, with the object of disposing of the land in ownership to the crofter tenants.

"One of the Crofters Commissioners visited Glendale in December for the purpose of discussing with the manager of the Board "certain final rearrangements to be effected before the sale of the property to the occupiers is completed". From this it may be gathered that the experiment of transferring the holdings to crofter proprietors is about to come into operation."

The above serves to illustrate the always close links that existed between the CDB and the Crofters Commission. The Commission chairman, Sheriff Brand,was after all a member of the CDB.

Kilmuir's crofters always resisted every attempt to persuade them to buy their holdings, and in 1908 the Congested Districts Board agreed that they would be able to continue as tenants. As noted above, crofters at Barra and Syre had originally agreed to buy their new holdings, but in 1912 would vote (and be allowed) to resume the status of tenants. Only the Glendale crofters were ultimately convinced by the argument they would be better off buying their holdings.

Land Raids & the Vatersay Purchase

In 1907 Sheriff David Brand, chairman of the Crofters Commission and hence also *ex officio* a member of the Board of the CDB, retired. He was replaced by Sheriff Neil Kennedy, a Sutherland man. Brand had given great service.

At this time Vatersay was becoming probably the most famous - or notorious - case in which the CDB found itself embroiled. Cottars and fishermen living in overcrowded conditions on Barra and Mingulay had been seeking land on Vatersay from the proprietor Lady Gordon Cathcart for many years without success, apart from the grant of a very small area of land to be used for growing potatoes. Many of these people's forebears had been evicted from Vatersay just two generations earlier. The island was now in the hands of one farmer.

During the early 1900s, in frustration, cottars had built huts on Vatersay in the first of several land raids. The full story of the Vatersay raiding is told in Ben Buxton's superb book *The Vatersay Raiders*. The upshot was that eventually, in 1908, having breached an interdict served upon them, the raiders were arrested and sent to Edinburgh for trial. They were given two-month prison sentences, but the case won them so much public sympathy that, the following year, the CDB felt compelled to purchase Vatersay from Lady Gordon Cathcart at a price greatly in her favour, to create crofts for the Barra and Mingulay people.

Idrigil and Dalbeg

The Congested Districts Board was established to make life better for people. That was its ethos and it was the public's perception of it. So when relations between it and the crofters of Idrigil, by Uig, Kilmuir, Skye, also turned sour in 1910, leading to more land raids, it was a disaster for its image.

Land raids were by now familiar in the Highlands - but to have one occur on a CDB property was very bad news.

In 1908 the farm of Scuddaburgh, just north of Idrigil, became vacant when the former tenant's lease expired and was not renewed. Local crofters were desperate to be given the land. However, when the case was referred to the Crofters Commission, the best arable land was withheld from them. It was thought this would make a good 'model farm' or large croft on which the latest cultivation techniques might be demonstrated. But the locals were having none of that and pressed for another assessment of the case.

Throughout 1909, there was much pent-up feeling among the Idrigil crofters about Scuddaburgh Farm, though there are few mentions of it in CDB files for that year. In 1910, following a further referral to the Crofters Commission, they were again thwarted: a lesser amount of land, but still 63 acres, was withheld. Land raids were threatened; consequently, an interdict was obtained by the CDB, forbidding such a raid. But the crofters went ahead – there were land raids in April and June 1910.

In August a sheriff-officer was sent to arrest eleven Idrigil crofters and bring them to Portree sheriff court for trial; he was attacked, along with the CDB's Land Manager Angus Mackintosh, who lived in Uig and who was ordered by his superiors to accompany the sheriff officer and help identify the wanted men. Days later, the eleven crofters came forward voluntarily after all, to stand trial for the breach of interdict in the spring – and were jailed pending heavy fines being paid.

Such was the public outcry that money for all the fines was contributed within days and the men were released. For the attack on the sheriff officer and preventing the issuing of his summons, which was known as a deforcement, a number of Idrigil people - mostly women - were brought to trial in October and fined. Their fines were also paid from monies pledged by the public.

Elsewhere there had been yet more land raids. In May 1909, cottars on Lewis raided the farm of Dalbeg to plant potatoes. *The Scotsman* reported: "Some time ago the cottars of Shawbost petitioned the Government for allotments on the lands of Dalbeg, and the cottars of Carloway asked for allotments on the lands of Dalmore, which together constituted one farm. The cottars elsewhere throughout Lewis have also been petitioning for holdings, and it is understood that the proprietor, Major Matheson, has consented to the breaking up into small holdings of the farm of Mangursta in Upper Uig."

The adjacent item in the same edition noted that CDB staff had gone over to Lewis to manage that project:

"Major Duncan Matheson's latest scheme is the breaking up of the farm of Mangursta, on the west side of the Lews, for the benefit of the 22 squatters in the township of Breanish. Two officials of the Congested Districts Board, Mr W.G.Coles, Engineer, and Mr A.MacKintosh, Land Manager, have been engaged for a number of days at Mangursta. .. It appears that the arable land is insufficient to provide suitable holdings for all the squatters, and it is possible that additional ground will be sought in the adjoining farm of Ardvoil. A few years ago Major Matheson proposed to settle these Breanish squatters on the farm of Dalmore, but the place was unfavourably reported upon by one of the Crofters Commissioners."

Dealing with Rent Arrears

While the above would seem to show the CDB taking positive steps on behalf of needy cottars, its annual report in 1909 illustrated that the Board would also take punitive action over crofters not paying their rent. The report noted:

"In a scheme of State-aided creation of new holdings, it is manifestly of the highest importance that the settlers should make punctual payment of the sums due by them. We regret to say that in the case of several estates the settlers, with some exceptions, are considerably in arrear. We thought it our duty to intimate that unless there was an immediate improvement in this respect, steps would have to be taken to enforce payment or to foreclose.

"The result of this intimation has not been satisfactory, and we have had to take proceedings in Court against certain selected defaulters, who, we have reason to believe, could have met their obligations in a much more satisfactory manner than they have done. The following statement shows how matters stand in each of the settlements formed on estates purchased by us:

	Syre	Barra	Glendale	Kilmuir	Total
Arrears at last term	£210	£227	£89	£2,483	£3,009
Amount due for last year	£540	£261	£649	£1,577	£3,027
Amounts paid last term	£223	£78	£621	£1,125	£2,047
Total overdue, 31.3.09	£527	£410	£117	£2,935	£3,989

The report noted that Kilmuir tenants were nearly £3,000 in arrears - roughly £6-£7 per crofter - and criticised crofters in regard to various practices, including the breeding and selling of livestock.

"We regret that, in many cases, it seems impossible to convince the owners of stock that they should retain for breeding purposes the best produce of our sires. The temptation to get an immediate good price induces too many of these owners to sell at the earliest moment the best animals they have, thus leaving them with the worst from which to breed.

"We have impressed upon Grazings Committees the importance of this question both as regards the present and in preparation for the time when our supply of good sires in a district must be modified or stopped."

Reading this, one wonders why crofters should not have expected the CDB to continue supplying them with bulls and rams. Why should they expect the practice to be "modified or stopped"? The assumption was that the crofters would one day be proprietors – and no longer liable for such assistance.

But did crofters not have a legitimate right to wish to remain as tenants and to receive such (fairly inexpensive) state assistance?

The CDB report even made the same point about the provision of seed, criticising crofters for expecting a fresh supply of seed to be given each year instead of propagating their own, and for not manuring their land properly, and for incessant cropping, which drained the ground of its fertility.

It also strongly criticised those crofters who kept overstocks of sheep, suggesting that soumings in each township needed to be checked and revised.

The report mentioned experiments in new cultivation techniques carried out on Skye by the Aberdeen & North of Scotland Agricultural College, which had yielded good results. The person responsible for such experiments, although not named, was undoubtedly Colin MacDonald, later to be the author of several sympathetic books about crofting including *Highland Journey*.

New Land Bill's Failure Damages the CDB

The incoming Liberal government of 1906 had tried in vain for several years to get a Small Landholder's Bill through parliament. That year, it was withdrawn before reaching a vote.

In the summer of 1907 a bill was passed in the Commons but withdrawn after a long debate in the House of Lords, where it was contentious among landowners (of whom there were many in that House).

Brought forward again in 1908, it passed with a huge majority in the Commons but was again rejected in the Lords, notably by Balfour of Burleigh, a previous Secretary for Scotland and first chairman of the CDB.

In late 1908 John Sinclair, Secretary for Scotland, suggested to the new Prime Minister Asquith that if he were to be ennobled and move to the Lords, he could monitor the progress of the bill in that House when it was brought forward again.

Two General Elections in 1910 were fought particularly on the question of reform of the House of Lords, which had so delayed this bill. The Small Landholders (Scotland) Bill finally became law after passing through both the Commons and the Lords in 1911 - with only limited opposition from the House of Lords after Prime Minister Asquith threatened to flood the House with 500 new peers.

These long delays in the passing of the bill had an unfortunate side-effect, in that throughout the country it was expected that the days of the Crofters Commission and Congested Districts Board were numbered. Crofters whom the CDB had been trying to persuade to purchase their holdings could see clearly that under the intended new legislation they could remain as tenants.

Furthermore, the Congested Districts Board itself was clearly paralysed by doubt as to the point of making land purchases. Indeed, after 1904 only two further purchases (of Vatersay and Seafield in Easter Ross) were made before the CDB was abolished in 1912.

The Act of 1911 was intended to address the land issue throughout Scotland, replacing the Congested Districts Board with a Board of Agriculture for Scotland with a much greater budget and increased powers to make compulsory purchases of land for crofter re-settlement. The Act was scheduled to come into force from 1st April 1912, when the Crofters Commission would also cease to exist, its functions being taken on by the new Scottish Land Court.

Before the new Act eventually came into force, the CDB declared in 1911 that all crofting parishes in Scotland - and not just those designated following the 1897 Act - were now considered as "congested." This had the effect of increasing the Board's own area of responsibility greatly.

Land Manager Angus MacKintosh was moved from Uig to Edinburgh, where he thereafter worked from CDB headquarters, making regular visits back to the Highlands. His departure from Uig was well publicised by the *People's Journal* of 17th December 1910, which included these pointed comments about a young local doctor, Grant Macdonald, who had lately arrived to work at the Martin Hospital in Uig. Dr Macdonald was meantime having to rent Conon Lodge near Uig, which was normally let out to shooting tenants by the CDB.

"His work has within a year made him a name throughout Skye; and his knowledge of Gaelic and his thorough sympathy with and comprehension of the Celtic mind render his remaining there a consummation devoutly to be wished. .. Surely the Board will for once take the patently wise counsel,, and try to attach him to the district by selling him one of the two houses that Mr MacKintosh's departure to Edinburgh will leave open."

The Court of the Dogs

In the last few weeks of the CDB's existence there occurred a memorable court case which became known afterwards as the Court of the Dogs or, in Gaelic, *Cùirt nan Con*. It ensured that the Congested Districts Board went out in a blaze of bad publicity.

As one of its final initiatives, the Board saw fit to make an issue of the number of dogs roaming on various Hebridean crofting estates without their owners having paid for a dog licence. By law, dogs used by farmers to manage livestock were exempt from being licensed. In 1907 the local sheriff had granted hundreds of exemptions to local crofters and cottars until early 1912. The CDB, realising that licence exemptions were shortly due for renewal, decided to act both for itself and, after consultations, for the four private estates between Barra and Harris. The case was heard at Lochmaddy, North Uist, on 13th March 1912.

Files on this case in CDB archives reveal that it originated in 1911, in a letter sent in June by a resident of Lochs to the newly-elected local MP, J.T.Macpherson.

"The Island is swarming with useless and dangerous dogs. A great many of these dogs belong to cottars who pay no licence for them and they cause great and serious injury to our lambs, and even the crofters' dogs kill the lambs right and left. We complained to the police but nothing was done by them, and the Procurator Fiscal says it is not his duty but the County Council's duty to bring the guilty parties to book. Surely we are entitled to protection against the damage done to our stock by these useless curs that roam over the Island. Some months ago a number of persons were in court for keeping dogs without licence and it had a great effect in making the owners drown their dogs, but they were people from the Point district only and nothing was done to summon others from other parts of the Island where dogs are more numerous. .. Someone must be compelled to summon the owners of these dogs or there will be no use in us keeping stock at all."

This letter was passed by Macpherson to the Secretary for Scotland, who asked Angus MacKintosh to consider the complaint. MacKintosh replied: "Similar complaints were made some time ago by crofters in some of the other outer islands on which members and officials of the CDB expressed their opinions. .. many of the crofters keep two dogs and even cottars keep one or more and as few of them are properly fed they are bound to roam about in search of food and to prey on weak sheep or lambs. I don't think the CDB can help. **The remedy is to stop the exemption** *certificates, except to herds and shepherds*, and to prosecute all who do not pay licences and whose dogs are found roaming about."

On 8th February 1912, Thomas Wilson made further running when he wrote to MacKintosh from Lochmaddy:

"Barra Dog Licence Exemptions. A couple of years ago, Sheriff Campbell decided that a crofting township farm was only entitled to have exempted from licence duty the same number of dogs as the law allowed exemption for on a farm with the same sheep stock – but that these existing licence holders were privileged till 1912. The period of privilege has now expired, and if objection is taken before the sheriff each crofting township will have no more exempt dogs than a similar farm would have. Objections fall to be lodged by 13th inst and I think the Board should take objection for its Barra properties.

"I expect most of the other Outer Island proprietors will lodge objections, as the exempt dog has become a nuisance both to crofters and proprietors. I have no doubt that when the wholesale exemptions of recent years is stopped, and crofters and cottars have to pay Licence Duty for their dogs, there will be a wholesale destruction of dogs and a corresponding good to crofters."

Following this, MacKintosh wrote to the CDB Secretary: "I certainly think the Board should lend their influence to oppose the promiscuous granting of Exemption Licences for crofters' dogs as has been done hitherto. For years I have been convinced that the greatest curse to the crofters' stock, and particularly to their sheep, is the exceptionally large number of half-starved dogs which are in every township, and which are generally allowed to roam at will. Lambs and weak sheep are always a prey to these animals. I once got a census made of the dogs in South Uist and I think there were over 1,300 in that one parish, almost all of which had exemption certificates. Not only did crofters get exemption for a dog, but cottars who had no land or stock but probably a patch of potatoes, were allowed to keep a dog to chase away other people's stock. Very few of those crofters really require to keep a dog, and only those who cannot very well do without one will pay licence. I think Mr Wilson should be instructed to oppose, on behalf of the Board, the further granting of exemption certificates."

The Secretary for Scotland Lord Pentland approved. On 15th February, Thomas Wilson wrote MacKintosh: "I have lodged objections for each of the CDB, Lady Cathcart, Sir Arthur Campbell-Orde and Lord Dunmore and have seen the sheriff who has arranged to deal with the applications and objections on 13 March. .. 1,753 applications for exemption from the Long Island have been lodged with the sheriff clerk, and a number have yet to come in."

Crofters came to the court hearing from all over the islands. The applications for exemption from the dog-licence fee were challenged in court by Thomas Wilson, who on this occasion was acting not only for the Congested Districts Board but, quite amazingly, for Lady Gordon Cathcart, owner of Barra and South Uist, as well as the North Uist estate of Sir Arthur Campbell-Orde and the Harris estates of Sir Samuel Scott and Lord Dunmore.

His opposite number, representing the crofters, was Alasdair Iain Macdonald. Colin Macdonald, who was a County Agricultural Adviser for the North of Scotland Agricultural College, recalled in *Highland Journey* that Thomas Wilson was widely known as the Factor Dubh. Formerly a champion of the crofters' cause in 1880s land agitation cases, and even in the early days of the CDB, Wilson was now seen by local crofters as being on the 'wrong' side..

"There was some 'preliminary sparring' by the lawyers," wrote Colin Macdonald, *"then the Factor Dubh made the case that there had been 'gross laxity' in the granting of exemptions from the licence. 'There were ten dogs on the Islands for every one required for the purpose which earned exemption in terms of the Act. These dogs were a menace to sheep and cattle, and a public nuisance.*

"He would argue before his Lordship that the vast majority of dog-owners in the Islands, being merely crofters, could not qualify for tax-exemption as farmers at all.' He asked the sheriff to find accordingly."

Angus MacLellan, one of the crofters affected, recalled in *The Furrow Behind Me* how Wilson pleaded that crofters had no need for dogs in such numbers as they were kept, and suggested three or four dogs be kept in every township - that would be sufficient.

Alasdair Macdonald responded by asking how the township would decide who was to keep a dog, suggesting every man would most likely vote for himself; if they were to cast lots to see who got a dog, the chances were 'the lot could fall on a bad man and a bad dog.'

It took Alasdair Macdonald just a few minutes to convince the Sheriff that all crofters were, in fact, farmers and that, therefore, their dogs should be exempt from needing a licence. In the event, only a small minority of the dog-owners present (those who were not crofters) were refused exemption from paying the licence.

On 20th March, Wilson wrote tersely to MacKintosh:

"At the Dog Exemption Court held at Lochmaddy last week – which I attended – Sheriff Campbell reversed the decision he gave in 1907 and held that any person was a farmer who had more than one cattle head, whether he held land lawfully or unlawfully, and as such was entitled to receive an exemption for a dog, if claimed.

"This was most unfortunate, as it completely upsets all endeavours to regulate dogs; for example, the Vatersay Common Grazings Committee held a meeting and agreed that four dogs was sufficient for all Vatersay and they nominated four persons to hold the exemptions – the Sheriff refused to give effect to the Common Grazings Committee finding, other five tenants from Vatersay having claimed exemptions, and granted all exemptions claimed from Vatersay. Three objections were sustained and

47 rejected from the (Congested Districts) Board's property. The Sheriff held us liable in expenses to successful claimants."

Colin MacDonald again: *"It was a great victory for the crofters and their lawyer Alasdair Macdonald. Expenses were awarded against the objecting parties in respect of each of Macdonald's clients, so there was just cause for a little celebration amongst us at the hotel that night. The bill for costs came to over £7,000."*

Donald Macintyre (known as *Domhnall Ruadh*) attended the court case as a very young representative of the South Uist township of Snishival. He later wrote a poem, *Triall gu Cùirt nan Con (The Journey to the Court of the Dogs)*, which was not so much about the case and its verdict, but about the hardships of the actual travelling which he and his colleagues had to undertake, crossing the south and north fords either side of Benbecula, just to reach the Court House at Lochmaddy.

* * *

Most CDB files include a number of lengthy annotations made by members of the Board among whom a report was circulated. This file, however, ends with a remarkable string of "Noted" and "Seen". There was perhaps little to be said. What Board members really thought of the sheriff whose verdict seemed to fly in the face of his earlier ruling was unrecorded and probably unprintable anyway.

However, faced with a thousand disgruntled crofters milling about outside Lochmaddy Court House, was it any wonder that the sheriff ruled as he did?

This was, in effect, a demonstration of crofter power. The people were standing up not only against the CDB but against what they surely perceived as an unholy alliance between it and Lady Gordon Cathcart and the other local lairds.

For that very good reason, this court case went down in folk history. The dog-licence debacle dealt a final blow to the reputation of the Congested Districts Board. It was amazing that the CDB should have liaised with the private estates in this case and challenged exemptions on their behalf; and also that it casually squandered thousands of pounds on bringing a case which it lost. Yet a difference in valuation of less than £25 had been the cause of months of stalemate between the Board and the Idrigil crofters over the Scuddaburgh Farm settlement.

Board of Agriculture succeeds Congested Districts Board

Less than three weeks after the Court of the Dogs, the Congested Districts Board ceased to exist on 1st April 1912 and its functions were taken over by the Board of Agriculture for Scotland. On the same day the Crofters Commission was replaced by the newly established Scottish Land Court.

The Board of Agriculture for Scotland had far greater powers than its predecessor and a much larger budget of £200,000 per annum, which was to be used in addition to any income arising from previous CDB activities: namely about £5,000 in annual rent, £1,500 in annual loan repayments, and an unused surplus of no less than £26,000.

The fact that the CDB had this surplus to hand so late in its financial year was exdraordinary, when its legally binding remit had been to spend its funding.

The new Board was required to deal with the whole of Scotland, unlike the CDB which, at least until 1911, had dealt only with the crofting counties. Some sections of the 1897 Congested Districts Act still remained in force.

There were three members on the new Board of Agriculture, with John Sutherland being in charge of the Land Division and designated the Commissioner for Small Holdings. He had various regional sub-commissioners and assistant sub-commissioners reporting to him.

Most beneficially, the Board of Agriculture enjoyed powers (which the CDB had never been given) to make compulsory purchases of land with a view to creating smallholdings. The procedure was that the Board of Agriculture's Commissioner for Small Holdings should try to agree on a proposed purchase of land with a proprietor, but if this approach failed he could then refer the case to the Board, which could apply to the Land Court, which in turn could insist on a compulsory purchase - also referring the case for compensation to an adjudicator appointed by the Court of Session.

By the end of 1912, the Board of Agriculture would receive no fewer than 3,370 applications for new holdings, including 1,300 from the Outer Hebrides. However, the Board's procedures proved inadequate to process such claims with the speed desired by applicants, and this resulted in further land raids in 1913, notably on South Uist and Lewis, where Reef farm was raided and the stock driven off. An interim interdict was obtained but, just as at Idrigil, it was broken; eleven cottars were convicted of breach of interdict in March 1914 and sentenced to six weeks in prison. On 1st April they agreed not to trespass on Reef again and were freed.

During the 1914-18 war the Board of Agriculture could do little in terms of breaking up estates and farms, but with the return of peace there was a general desire that ex-servicemen and their families should have the land they needed in the Highlands.

The *Land Settlement (Scotland) Act* of 1919 at last gave the Board of Agriculture full powers of compulsory purchase in acquiring land to create or enlarge crofts.

The Congested Districts after World War One

Meanwhile the term *"Congested Districts"* remained current even under the Board of Agriculture. For example in its report for 1922 under *"Public Works in Congested Districts"*, the Board noted that various projects had been assisted: £2,800 had been allocated to works on the Portree-Broadford road, £2,300 to Badentarbet Pier in Coigach, £1,000 to the Inverbroom-Loggie Road and a small sum to maintaining St Kilda pier, among various projects.

A section in this report headed *"Vote for the Relief of Unemployment and Distress – Road Schemes in the Outer Hebrides"* described how Parliament had voted funds to be allocated to areas suffering acute hardship in post-war Britain, with the Board of Agriculture delegated to spend the money allocated to the Hebrides. During March 1922, 2,700 men of Lewis and Harris were employed on making roads, the work being organised through Township Committees, and £40,000 was spent on such projects in the year.

Regarding land settlement schemes, that report noted that the long-awaited purchase of Raasay and Rona had been concluded "and the Board are now the owners of the surface, but not of the mineral rights. Owing to pressure of work on other schemes, and also owing to an outbreak of typhus on Raasay, making it inadvisable to introduce fresh settlers, the Board have settled only seven applicants on the arable portions of their proposed holdings, and have retained the management of the remainder of the lands in their own hands. It is hoped to complete the settlement early in 1923, when 30 to 40 applicants may be given entry."

During the Board of Agriculture's first ten years (since April 1912) it had created 1,237 new holdings in the crofting counties, as follows: 243 in Argyll; 174 in Caithness; 52 on mainland Inverness-shire; 139 on Skye; 32 on Harris; 26 on North Uist; 110 on South Uist; 67 on Barra; 72 on mainland Ross-shire, 187 on Lewis; 68 in Sutherland; 22 on Orkney; and 45 on Shetland.

In Scotland as a whole the Board had created 1,953 new holdings - therefore nearly two thirds had been allocated in the crofting counties. There had also been 1,234 enlargements to croft-holdings in the crofting counties, which was over 99% of all enlargements made.

These allocations were divided into those for ex-servicemen and civilians – the Land Settlement (Scotland) Act of 1919 having put a priority on giving land to those returning from the First World War.

The Board's 1923 report noted that it had now acquired over 350,000 acres of Scotland since 1912, of which just over 9% was arable land, and the rest grazing. The Board additionally owned the six properties inherited from the CDB (Barra, Syre, Glendale, Kilmuir, Vatersay and Seafield).

The Board had recently bought the 9,500 acre estate of Kilbride, on Strath, Skye, using powers of compulsory purchase under the 1919 Land Settlement Act. "It was found possible without resort to arbitration to reach agreement with each of the tenants on the four farms of the estate as to the settlement of his claim for compensation, and entry to the farms was taken at Martinmas 1923. Arrangements are being made for the formation of 26 new holdings and 30 enlargements of existing holdings." At Galson, Lewis, 52 new holdings had been formed during 1923 as a result of a compulsory purchase of the land.

This annual report also reported a remarkable scheme of voluntary migration from the Western Isles to Skye: "In connection with the subdivision of their Bracadale estate (Skye), it may be of interest to mention that the Board, in an endeavour to relieve to some extent the prevailing congestion in Lewis and Harris, are carrying out a scheme of migration from these islands to the northern portion of the farm of Talisker, on which 70 holdings are being formed for the benefit of applicants of the fisherman-crofter type. Up to the end of the year, 51 ex-service applicants had taken up occupation, 39 of these being from Harris."

"Agrarian unrest" was reported among cottars who wanted land, with land raids at Strathaird, Skye, where six men were sentenced to two months imprisonment for breach of interdict; and at Kilbride, where two men got 25 days imprisonment.

In July 1923 the Secretary for Scotland had issued a Statutory Order to speed up procedures for the compulsory purchase of land under the Land Settlement Act.

Under certain sections of the 1897 Congested Districts Act which were still in force, this report noted that loans had been made to eight Glendale crofters for house improvements.

Under *"Loans to Fishermen,"* the Board of Agriculture noted that it had acquired 484 acres of land from the common grazings at Cross, Swanibost, Habost and Lionel, on Lewis, to create 135 two-acre plots for use as house sites and for cultivation at a rental of ten shillings a year. 42 applicants had already been settled: "31 of these being 'squatters' already on the ground."

In a section entitled *"Public Works in the Congested Districts"*, further grants were noted, for example for work on Broadford Pier and the Bays of Harris road. In 1923, over £12,000 had been spent on projects to relieve unemployment and distress in the Outer Hebrides through further road-building projects.

In the 1930 report of the (now) Department of Agriculture for Scotland, it was announced that 13 extra staff had been taken on in the Land Division "partly with a view to the acceleration of land settlement operations."

It was noted that the Board of Agriculture now owned 415,000 acres of Scotland, comprising 103 estates (of which six had been taken over from the CDB). A report on Kilmuir compared the estate with how it was in 1904, when acquired by the CDB: the area under crofting tenure was now 44,600 acres (compared to 24,332 in 1904); there were 441 crofts (against 356); 45 townships (up from 35); while the number of farms had dropped from ten to none.

Another special report in 1930 concerned Syre and made the same comparisons with how it had been when taken on by the CDB - there were now 21 families living in Syre as against two previously; the population was 95 as against 10; and 232 acres were cultivated, as compared with just 6 acres in 1904. The number of cattle had increased from 4 to 158, sheep from 1,700 to 2,163, and horses from none to 26.

48

The Board of Agriculture's report for 1930 also included a brief account of the final evacuation of St Kilda.

From these 1930 statistics it was apparent that, at last, too late in the day, the Board of Agriculture was making proper inroads into the huge task of crofter re-settlement.

Finlay J.Macdonald recalls the Board of Agriculture

In his autobiography *Crowdie and Cream*, author and broadcaster Finlay J.Macdonald recalled his boyhood in the late 1920s on Harris, where many years earlier the people had been ruthlessly evicted from the rich arable land of the south-west onto the rockier land fringing the northern and eastern coasts.

At last the Board of Agriculture was turning its attention to Harris and allocating new croft holdings at Scarista.

"My father and seven others were lucky. .. All they had to do was pay their small rentals of about seven pounds a year, build themselves a village, and build, each to himself, a family of children and a flock of sheep in whichever order he chose."

For Finlay's father it was a return to the promised land, his ancestors having been evicted from South Harris. But life would still be tough.

"He was not to know that he was not escaping from bondage but, rather, going into it."

MacDonald's family stayed in one end of the old schoolhouse while his father was building the new family croft-house. Crofting was hard, and he depicted the Board of Agriculture's staff as being unaware of the realities of the lifestyle.

"Doubtless some ex-colonial bureaucrat, who had moved his desk from one of the crumbling outposts of empire to Edinburgh, would ... consider that a grateful government had done well by eight men returning from the trenches or the navy."

He recalled his family's patient wait for building materials brought by the puffer *Dunara Castle*, and the visits of the officials of the Board to inspect progress on new croft houses:

"Occasionally, word would get round the community that 'men from the Board were coming round'. These were always men wearing knickerbockers who travelled in pairs, whose morning coffees and afternoon teas arrived on their desks at the pre-ordained times regardless of whether or not the *Dunara Castle* was being held up in Castlebay for nine days by a force ten gale."

Ahead of such visits, the locals would get wind and make sure that they were busy at work on their houses "as the government's hired car jolted its way down the road, stopping here and there to justify its journey. .. the crofters, who could modulate the fluency of their English as the occasion demanded, were always cautiously reassuring .. And at the end of the inspection, they always wished the officials 'a nice holiday' ".

Nevertheless, the overall purpose of the Board of Agriculture was a fit and proper one, as MacDonald acknowledged: *"What an earlier Irish politician had described in similar circumstances as 'the unshirkable duty to strive towards undoing the unnatural divorce between the people and the land.'"*

Highlighting how difficult the Board had found it to get hold of land for re-settlement in its earlier years, the author recalled a joke of the time.

" 'What is that floating in the ebb?' the old Highlander asked his crony. 'It looks like a board of wood or something.'

'If it is moving fast,' was the reply, 'it will be a plank of wood. If it's moving slowly, it'll be the Board of Agriculture.' "

If ever you wanted to read a justification for the crofting way of life and its value in preserving a culture and turning out the finest of people, you could do no better than read Finlay J.MacDonald's book.

The Congested Districts Board in Retrospect

Reviewing the work of the Congested Districts Board in 1918, the author J.P.Day was scathing in his assessment of its record on land settlement. He noted that, at the close of its fifteen-year existence, the Board claimed to have created or helped to create 640 new holdings as well as having enlarged 1,138 crofts.

The endeavours of the Board could be assessed in four key categories, all of which were part of its original remit: (a) its purchases of land and resale in small holdings; (b) its cooperation with proprietors willing to subdivide farms; (c) aiding migration; (d) its aid for the formation of fishermen's holdings and the erection of fishermen's dwellings.

"It is possible to say at once," wrote Day, *"that all except (b) were complete failures. It is a matter of considerable doubt whether the Board's experiments succeeded even in showing that, given a generous amount of assistance at the start, crofters could be established in new small holdings in a self-supporting and economically independent position."*

His criterion for judging the experiment was cold economics.

"If the purpose of the State (in purchasing land) was to prove that proprietors could without loss break up their farms, and establish small holdings for the surplus crofting population, it is abundantly clear that this purpose was not achieved."

But Day inadvertently second-guessed how posterity (we today) would come to view the importance of the crofting way of life to the West Highlands:

"If, on the other hand, the purpose was merely to relieve the congestion by providing land, this, of course, was done to the extent shown."

This author seemed not to recognise that the providing of land had, in fact, been the key moral imperative behind the Congested Districts Board Act of 1897. Anyone who understood what hardship so many people in the Highlands had suffered in the

18th and 19th centuries would have felt, then as now, that whatever could be done to support them in the early years of the 20th century should have been done.

The Congested Districts Board was set up all wrong. It did not have the power to effect compulsory purchases of land, it should have been given a proper budget rather than the inadequate £35,000 which it had at its disposal, and it had no full-time Gaelic-speaking staff. It could and should have done much more to help the survival of a people and a culture.

There have been people and institutions in West Highland history which prompt the thought "Thank God for them" – the Crofters Commission and the Hydro Board come to mind. But alas, the Congested Districts Board is not one. No doubt its staff were well-meaning. But if only it had been headed up by a charismatic, radically-minded figure. Admittedly, public bodies do not usually produce such figures. But the CDB could have tried to recruit such a man - someone who might have earned the people's confidence in his Board. Several members of the Irish CDB had had this effect, and the Irish CDB also had a proper budget, of over £200,000 after 1909.

John MacLeod wrote in *Highlanders* of the period around the end of the 19th century: "What West Highlanders clamoured for was a programme of resettlement: the recovery of deer forest and sheepwalks, and the resurrection of old crofting communities. The Congested Districts Board greatly preferred – was better endowed with the appropriate powers – to create employment opportunities, in fishing, agriculture and industry. Like .. such bodies, then and since, it was quite capable of significantly improving the Highland standard of living; *it failed, utterly, to address the region's fundamental problems.*"

There needed to be the political will during the mid-1890s, either within the Liberal government which was in power until 1895, or within the Tory government which followed it, to recognise the findings of the Red Deer Commission which had identified huge acreages of land as suitable to be turned into either crofters' arable land or grazing land. Those acreages should have been cited in the CDB's legislation as the basis of legally binding, ambitious but attainable targets for re-settlement, using powers of compulsory purchase.

The CDB's legally constituted purpose might have included, for example, the creation of 25,000 crofts of ten acres each, along with a million acres of common grazing land, the result to be a settled crofting population of 100,000 people, who would bring much cleared land back under cultivation and who could consequently live self-sufficient, productive lives. Two per cent of the Scottish population might thus have become tenants of nine per cent of Scottish land. It would have been a good deal for them and for the country.

Ewen A.Cameron noted of the CDB: *"Over the course of its existence, the outlook of the CDB seemed all too often to be at odds with that of the crofters."*

Still, it must be acknowledged that many townships benefited from CDB grants towards specific improvements, including the provision of boat-slips, piers, and harbours. The Board gave aid for the breeding of livestock and, by the end of its lifetime, had purchased 679 bulls and 2,378 rams, all usefully lent to grazing committees for breeding. Poultry farming was encouraged, as was the growing of vegetables and potatoes; potato seed was supplied and there were experiments in spraying potatoes with chemicals. There were grants for local shows, and the CDB assisted in developing home industries, including the making of tweed.

Angus MacLeod, who belonged to Pairc, in Lochs, Lewis, recalled with humour the bulls which were provided annually to crofting townships:

"... they were referred to as 'congested bulls' (tarbh a congestic), which was a Highland beast with two large horns like a bicycle handlebars. In our youth we equated the Highland breed of cattle with the word 'congestick'."

It was not that the Congested Districts Board did no good. It was just that it did not do nearly as much good as it should have done. It was a tragic failure.

* * *

Writing in *Highland Journey* in 1943, Colin MacDonald summarised the benefits of the crofter's way of life, along with its drawbacks and what needed to be done:

"It is now a matter of general comment among young people in both town and country that a job in a city is a very uncertain thing. Conversely, many of them have come to appreciate the solid advantages that go with life on the land. To a young countryman a job at three or four pounds per week looked wealth. Now, in the city he knows that even when such a wage is assured it has a habit of vanishing in umpteen ways .. and he realises he would be much better off in the country, earning a quarter of that amount in addition to the potatoes and milk and butter and cream and poultry and eggs and the dozen other substantial things which he could produce on his own holding.

"He also knows that in the city he is more or less of a serf, while on his holding he is a king in his castle.

"If I were asked to state in two words the improvements which would do more than any other to make life on the land in the Highlands more attractive these words would be roads and houses. Not merely main roads, but roads - and good roads - to and through every glen and clachan and croft, and my houses would be of attractive design, with hot and cold water and electric light and power."

The latter requirements - electric light and power - were about to be addressed. A generation after the Congested Districts Board had ceased to exist, Tom Johnston showed what a difference real leadership could make, by helping to secure far-reaching legislation which led to the formation of the North of Scotland Hydro-Electricity Board in 1944.

The Hydro Board would bring employment to remote areas in the years to come - and eventually provide electricity to almost every Highland house. Johnston had started out as a radical, anti-establishment, campaigning journalist at the time the CDB was in operation. He was subsequently elected as an MP, and became Secretary of State for Scotland in 1941.

Crofting has been through many upheavals since the days of the CDB, and the debate about its future goes on. The Crofters Act of 1955 re-established a Crofters Commission, in Inverness, which took over most of the functions of the Department of Agriculture in regard to crofting matters, although its powers are now again shifting towards Edinburgh. The new Commission was not, however, the same as the original Crofters Commission of 1886-1912, whose functions were and are largely those of the modern Scottish Land Court.

It is thanks to the survival of the crofting way of life that a resident population was sustained in the West Highlands at a crucial period around the turn of the last century.

There has been a lot to be thankful for in recent decades. At the eleventh hour, Gaelic culture has grown confident of itself again, thanks largely to campaigners whose vision helped establish the Gaelic college Sabhal Mòr Ostaig on Skye, BBC Alba, and Gaelic-medium education. There is a flourishing literature in Gaelic.

The columns of the *West Highland Free Press*, inspired by Brian Wilson, have shaped the thinking of a couple of generations, particularly on the land issue, as have the writings of historians and authors including James Hunter (who also played a key role in the Scottish Crofters' Union), Ewen A.Cameron, Roger Hutchinson (also of the *Free Press*), Tom Devine and Andy Wightman. Their writings have been as important in the modern era as the writings of Alexander Mackenzie and John Murdoch were a century earlier.

Community land buyouts in the last twenty years have seen people in various parts of the West Highlands regain significant control over their own destinies.

The Highland Clearances, and the lairds and factors involved in them, left a horrible stain on Scottish history. It is thanks to those who stood up for the interests of the ordinary Highlander, from John Murdoch onwards, that the legacy of the Clearances is not simply empty glens and straths.